EUROPE

ASCENDANT

*The International Politics
of Unification*

3

EUROPE

ASCENDANT

The International Politics
of Unification

BY

GEORGE LISKA

The Johns Hopkins Press, Baltimore, Md.

This book has been brought to publication with the
assistance of a grant from The Ford Foundation.

FOR THOSE

OF WHOM

I DO NOT SPEAK

Y penser toujours. . . .

Preface and
Acknowledgments

This essay is a companion piece to *Nations in Alliance: The Limits of Interdependence,* published by The Johns Hopkins Press in 1962. It elaborates upon a problem which is treated only casually in the earlier book, the problem of an intimate association among sovereign states in general and Western European states in particular. The essay is self-contained in regard to its central theme; but as a statement on contemporary politics and strategies in the Atlantic area and in the world at large it can be critically judged only in conjunction with the earlier, more technical work which it supplements.

Some of the inspiration for this book goes back to my stay in France and North Africa in 1962, a stay that was made possible by a grant of The Rockefeller Foundation. While in Paris, I enjoyed the advantages of association with the Centre d'Etude des Relations Internationales of the Fondation Nationale des Sciences Politiques, and the hospitality of the Centre Universitaire International.

The results of the specifically subsidized inquiry were published separately under the title *The Greater Maghreb: From Independence to Unity?* and are summarized in one section of this book. I actually wrote the book under the auspices of the Washington Center of Foreign Policy Research in the period between December, 1962, when I presented an outline of my central thesis to one of the Center's Round Tables, and late May, 1963, when the manuscript went to the publishers. I saw the manuscript through the press while teaching international politics at Wesleyan University and chose to leave it substantially unchanged despite intervening events.

I wish to express my appreciation to all the institutions that in one way or another promoted my work. I am especially grateful to Professor Arnold Wolfers, Director of the Washington Center, an affiliate of The Johns Hopkins School of Advanced International Studies, who helped make my stay a fruitful one; to Professor Robert W. Tucker, who read probingly the first version of the manuscript; to Miss Elizabeth Stabler, who edited a large part of the manuscript; and to all those former colleagues in the Center who listened to my oral arguments and discussed them with me on two separate occasions.

GEORGE LISKA

December, 1963

Contents

ix

CHAPTER IV

CONCLUSIONS

Introduction

A New Beginning

Europe, so often buried in the past thirty years, is very much alive again. What passed for irremediable decline may have been merely a crisis of renewal. Signs are accumulating that Europe may not re-enact the fate of Greece; that, if she so wills, she may again rise to the sense of direction and self-reliance that are the bases of all other lasting achievement.

There is no greater drama in international politics than the rise and decline of nations and powers. The drama is at its height during a period of major changes in the nature of international actors and relations among them. Such appears to be the present moment. The resumed progression in Europe has not been limited to her western part; but it is there that it has reached a critical point one-half century after the beginning of the continent's decline, and one-half millennium after the emergence of Europe as a secular system of separate states from the fabric of medieval unity. The years between 1914 and 1964 have witnessed the economic and political decay of the continent, its military degradation, and the bid of new powers for integral succession to the old. In the same time span lie similarly abortive bids in favor of new international politics to supplant traditional ways of

1

conducting relations among nations, identified with Europe and allegedly discredited in Europe.

It begins to appear that the European countries as they renew themselves will play a leading role in the fusing of the old and the new in international relations. This is as it should be. The reawakening of Europe to consciousness of her economic strength and her political and military potential takes place in a world that is both novel and familiar, at once the old European system of states writ large and a new world in which would-be successors to Europe grapple with the outsized problems that originated in the destructive wars and the inventive minds of the Europeans. The unity of Europe itself is being forged by means and forces that blend novelty in design with strategies informed by the perennial principles of statecraft.

In the following essay recent events in Europe and in the North Atlantic Alliance are placed in a historical perspective, and Western European developments are examined in a geographic compass enlarged to include North Africa and, tangentially, Eastern Europe and Communist China. In order to link the past with the present and open a perspective onto the future, the essay will draw heavily on historical analogy. If an analogy is to be meaningful for the analysis of statecraft, it must not be limited to the plausible sequences of crisis and *détente,* wartime disintegration and peacetime reconstruction, revolution and conservation. It must also be solicited for the lesser phenomena of implementation—the strategies chosen to carry out policy. Between social events, the art of comparison rests on a judicious identification of function concealed under the confusing welter of diversity in outward form and in episodic fact. When the realm is one of politics and policy, a heightened awareness of what is feasible in the active realm must control selection from among many half-way plausible analogies. But, in return, the ultimate rightness of the analysis rests on a marriage of insight with the will to transform historical precedent into a contemporary event. To illuminate possible continuities is not to predict necessary sequences. An essay for the present which invokes the past is not only a record of trends. It is also a documented plea for action of a particular kind.

CHAPTER I

The World
After a Half-Century

Just before the outbreak of World War I, the central position of Europe in world affairs was affirmed by two interrelated developments. The process of German national unification culminated in the rise of an economic and military superpower in the heart of the continent. And the global colonial diversion that owed much to the recasting of the post-Napoleonic equilibrium by Bismarck exhausted itself. Half a century later, one more global diversion from deadlock in Europe, consisting this time of competition over the political benefits of decolonization, has been apparently coming to a close. But the unification and consolidation of a great power at the nerve center of the world system is only a prospect, not yet a reality. An outline of the global setting of European unity may now usefully precede the sorting out of the immediate conditions of such unity, an effort which will broaden out again into the larger, global theme as we reach the end of the undertaking.

Global and Continental Horizons

The swing back and forth between continental and global horizons is one of the commonplaces of European diplomacy. Europe and the world outside were loosely linked since the age of the great discoveries and have been inter-connected strategically since the world wars of the mercan-tilist age. The interconnection has at all times reflected the relationship between the balance of trade and the balance of power, both determinants of varying configurations of co-operation and conflict.

The big contests of the seventeenth and eighteenth cen-turies were between France and Spain and France and Brit-ain; the key stakes were the monopoly of power in Europe and monopoly of trade in the Americas. The Franco-British duel culminated when, at mid-point between the global wars of the eighteenth and twentieth centuries, Napoleon was driven into continental conquests by his inability to con-quer England on the Afro-Asian battlefields of Alexander the Great or by an agreement with Alexander of Russia to turn the weapon of trade against England. At the end of the nineteenth century, Europe was still the principal subject of world politics, while the stakes and, to a large extent, the stage of great-power politics were once again in the non-European, colonial world. In 1914 Western Europe had again become the stage and the immediate stake of world politics, while remaining the subject. Germany was seeking world empire at the expense of Britain's second on the same battlefields where Britain had won much of her first—the battlefields of Northwestern Europe. In the period preceding World War I Germany was foremost among the continental powers in trying to reduce the preponderance of Britain in the world at large into something like equilibrium, without running the risks of a preliminary bid for supremacy in Europe. The risks of the preliminary bid were accepted, reluctantly or not, in 1914, when the global diversion had failed to reduce Britain's sway.

In the mid-1940's, Europe became the principal stage and the stake of the struggle between the United States and the Soviet Union. An American predominance in Europe would consummate the global preponderance which World War II conferred upon the United States, while dominance over Europe would enable the Soviets to wrench world power from America. In the 1950's, just as in the last years of the nineteenth and the first years of the twentieth centuries, there was a major diversion of political attention to the non-European world. Once again, this diversion relieved the tensions arising out of the deadlock of usable political-military power on the continent and coincided with a period of economic expansion within Europe. The two major global diversions were partially beneficial to Europe. The same cannot be said of a minor one in the 1930's, which was attended by economic depression and was altogether harmful to the political equilibrium of Europe. Fascist Italy, blocked in Central-Eastern Europe, tried to supplement prestige with power in the Mediterranean and Africa; she only made easier the general loss of both to Nazi Germany.

By 1964 the political opportunities presented by decolonization to its direct and indirect beneficiaries have been apparently on the wane. Western Europe was still, or was again indisputably, the chief stake as well as the stage of high policy. But it is no longer, or not immediately, the control over the continent by one of the superpowers that is at stake; it is rather the international orientation of Western Europe and the global configuration into which Europe would eventually fit herself, rather than be fitted. Western Europe is again becoming a subject of world politics and is getting ready to determine her fate as a stake and her use as a stage of co-operation and conflict.

Both the French and the German military empires finally had to fight in Europe if they were to remove the main support from Britain's global supremacy by overthrowing the European equilibrium. The fact that they had to fight on the continent can be regarded as the aboriginal curse lying on the land powers facing an island power in command of the seas; or the fact that the Germans, in particular, fought as they did can be regarded as the expression of self-defeating impatience to pluck the fruit of hegemony before the appointed season. But the continental jousts can also express a justifiable belief. The operation of the balance of power in the rationally structured universe of European politics has made victory, in any bid for dominance, difficult to the point of being virtually impossible. But, and this is the core of such a belief, to divert the struggle from Europe to the inadequately structured and charted outer world rules out not only decisive victory but also a rationally definable and manageable contest.

The return of diplomatic concern to Europe before World War I contributed to the tightening of bipolarity between the Central and the Entente powers. By contrast, a Western Europe united around the finally reconciled France and Germany and retaining a key position in much of Africa might help to relax further the contemporary polarization between the two adversary blocs. It would be rash to take such a development for granted, however. A revival of differences between France and Germany might thwart the present prospects of *détente* in conditions of greater security and independence for the states in both halves of Europe. When an earlier design for a continental league—at the time of Britain's global ascendancy and, specifically, her military involvement in South Africa—failed to materialize over

Franco-German differences, it effectively removed the only, feeble, chance of reversing the incipient polarization of Europe.

Our Victorian Age

Amid attention-absorbing crises, we can perceive the outlines of something vaguely resembling the Victorian Age, not for all men and states, but for the industrial nations of the northern hemisphere. The coming era might be called "Victorian" because conditions begin to recall those of late nineteenth-century Europe, with the difference, perhaps, that the industrialized nations may this time win victory over themselves rather than over each other.

Like the historical period that is named after the Queen of England and Empress of India, ours is a post-revolutionary period of growth and consolidation that precedes the next but not imminent phase of climactic confrontation. The earlier revolutionary period was marked by the wars of Napoleon and the social upheavals that attended and followed upon them; the more recent one culminated in the war with the Axis and witnessed subsequent upheavals in the social fabric and in the global balance of power. The earlier political and military crisis spread from France as the later one did from Germany; the earlier social unrest fanned out from England as the later one did from Russia. The nineteenth-century interlude between total wars saw the appeasement of social ferment in the key countries through the combined effect of sweeping economic growth and cautious political conservation. The political ferment was kept within bounds through an intermittent concert of powers based on a balance of both old and new power. The same methods appear to be fated to work out similar results for the same ancient countries, flanked and confined now by the new powers of North America and of Eurasia. The interlude is again marked by rapid evolution in the technology of weapons, forging the means of the next confrontation. It is again attended by rearrangements in the global political balance of power which set the stage and identify the actors of such a confrontation.

What are, briefly stated, the salient analogies between Victoria's age and our own? The two eras are, as we have already noted, ages of industrial growth and concentration. The industrial revolution had first galvanized England and spread from there to the European continent. Continuing a reversal that began imperceptibly at the height of the Victorian age and has since been confirmed by the upheavals and innovations attending and following both world wars, the industrial revolution has now moved into a still more grandiose phase on the continent. The latest economic transformation is now reaching out toward England, repaying a debt and settling a long-outstanding account. It may yet reshape in a comparable manner the relations of Western Europe with England's younger cousin on the other side of the Atlantic.

Both the Victorian age and our own are periods of unification. The focal point of these unifications was and is Germany; and the abortive or, at best, inconclusive phase of liberal-constitutional efforts toward unity is now again being succeeded as it was before by more forceful unifying strategies. These strategies extend into the unification process the spirit of non-ideological realism and the forms of personal diplomacy that reasserted themselves in all foreign-policy making in the second halves of the two centuries. Whereas the critical split in the earlier post-revolutionary period was one within states between Disraeli's two nations, the more recent one has been between groups of states clustered around two nuclear powers. Success in foreign policy became the imperative of survival, first for ruling classes and now also for leading states; the increasingly complex operations could not be jeopardized by distractions flowing from a meaningful participation of the public in ways other than protests against actual or alleged atrocities and the acclaim of real or synthetic heroes.

The international political system is currently marked, as it was in the comparable moment of the preceding century, by frantic diplomatic activity at the center of the world-power contest and by carefully calculated tests of strength at the peripheries. The two Korean crises, separated by a half-century, differ in detail and circumstance. But Russia may finally lose also the second contest and be pushed back upon Europe from Asia, while America's half-victory will be lastingly secured against half-defeated China only as won, in proxy this time, for Japan. The Laoses of today are being built up into buffer states on the model of the Siam of yesterday, until the trend forces Thailand back into the stance of Siam. Iran is no less embattled than was Persia in the tug of war between the successors to the Russian Tsars and to Imperial Britain. Despite the change in internal authority and in the source of the external threat, India is still threatened from the north. If the United States has replaced the United Kingdom in most of Asia and the Near East, Soviet Russia has replaced Imperial France and Imperial Germany in probing America's Monroe Doctrine in the Caribbean.

The involvements of the great powers in small, localized

wars and in the chase after concessions and influence marked both periods, as did the seemingly incongruent exchanges of reassuring whispers between the main actors in the wings of the central diplomatic stage. The concessions have borne upon the right to build hospitals or steel mills in return for political influence or military presence, whereas before they bore upon the building of railways for speedy movement of commerce and of foreign or foreign-trained local armies. The bases sought in the aftermath of World War II were for instruments of war traveling in inner and outer space, while before World War I they were for the armed watchdogs of the sea and of seaborne commerce. But naval power has re-emerged in both the Near and the Far East as a key component of the winning combination of military and economic means of influence and intervention, linked together by prudently daring diplomacy.

In both periods the readily usable economic and military instruments of political strategies were precariously contained by the concurrent arms race for military deterrent and political *Allianzwert,* or alliance value. The dreadnoughts of the Anglo-German naval competition that marked the passing of the Victorian age have become the thermonuclear weapons of the later age. In both instances, erroneous projections of a presumed capacity to produce ships or missiles into future ratios and gaps envenomed the arms race; and neither of the arms races could be attenuated by mutual inspection of key installations—shipbuilding yards before and testing grounds more recently. The faulty projections were alarming to the leading power of the day on grounds of morale as well as of military substance; the schemes for inspection were unacceptable to the upcoming power on grounds of prestige regardless of the capacity or will for subterfuge. It is possible, finally, that the new absolute weapons will be of as limited a use in a war they may help provoke, rather than prevent, as were the capital ships of yesterday.

The leading Western power of the day, the United Kingdom then and now the United States, had to cope with a major question: How to phase relations with the principal allied or protected countries with regard to the ultimate and the conventional weapons? The problem was approached by Britain through stages that may yet be repeated in full by the United States. At the outset, Britain virtually bartered effective military protection for rigid obedience by imperial wards. In the course of the nineteenth century Britain adopted a policy of transferring responsibility for local conventional defense to individual wards, concurrently with their progress in self-government. She did not proceed all the way to a federal organization of the empire, and she reserved for herself the exclusive control as well as the main financial burden of the principal shield and sword, the Navy. Only in a later phase did Britain finally accept with some reluctance a tacit partnership in naval power with the United States, the most eminent and most spectacularly emancipated and self-governing former dependency.

In essence, both periods—the Victorian and our own—were those of testing: testing of political nerve and resolve in the build-up of major forces and in seemingly back-breaking domestic spending; testing of new strategies and weapons in marginal wastes and deserts and in colonial and civil conflicts. The fate and future of the system rest suspended on the question whether a limited war can be fought also at the heart-center of the system. Germany is still the stake; Russia's estimate of the relation of forces among the powers and of her own chances of peaceful paramountcy in Europe (through Germany's indebted friendship) was the decisive factor in the 1860's and is again in the 1960's. The fact that the conflict *was* limited in 1870–71, if only in the sense of being localized, gave a new impetus to the global hegemony of Europe while sowing the seeds of her later downfall. The necessity to draw consequences from the fact that such a war may *not* be susceptible to limitation in 1970 may yet constitute the decisive turning point in Europe's decline and in the contemporary struggle for global hegemony.

The Struggle for the Succession to Europe

The global war from which the industrialized world has now recovered was the second Europe-centered global war for hegemony in the twentieth century; its counterpart in the preceding comparison was the Napoleonic conflagration. For the non-industrialized world of Afro-Asia, the same postwar period was one of resurgence rather than recovery, as more countries were able to assume the inheritance of Europe's colonial empires—with ease or only after bloody turmoil and with greater or lesser material profit. The events which this experience recalls are the eighteenth-century contests for successions.

The emancipated smaller states of the non-European world regard themselves as protagonists of the latest and most inspiring revolutionary principle. They found on this fact their claim to international role and influence. Such claims were advanced before, notably after World War I, as the decline of empire pursued its eastward course in Europe, and were temporarily allowed to stand. But the international influence of the lesser powers is likely to decline whenever rival great powers gravitate toward means of competition that do not entail their playing up of lesser states against one another. Again and again, following the Peace of Westphalia, the most small-state conscious of the great powers, France, abandoned the policy of small-state patronage both during her expansionist and her defensive periods and opted for accommodation among the great. There is no reason why Soviet Russia and the United States should act otherwise, once the small-state card has been played and has failed to bring nearer a successful termination of the contest for either. The emergence of a strong Western Europe will tend to reduce further the international standing of the most recent small-state protagonists of revolutionary anti-colonialism, mainly by creating new possibilities in the relations among the great powers and introducing chastened imperial experience into the relations between the small powers and at least one of the great. It is unlikely that global activism of a revolutionary but still destitute China could meaningfully revitalize the Communist option for many of the less developed countries. As confidence in the virtues of a mobile foreign policy declines, the next generation of inward-turned parochial politicians, military men, or economically-minded pragmatists can be expected to replace at an accelerated rate the older generation of foreign-policy oriented charismatic leaders in the new countries.

This trend will be fortunate, not least for the less developed countries themselves. A true emancipation of Europe's former Afro-Asian wards lies in the future; it cannot really begin before the leaders of the newly independent countries free themselves of their misconceptions about the

world and their role in it. The misconceptions were engendered by the constraints imposed upon others by the
bipolarity attending the world-wide diffusion of nominal
statehood in the colonial realm; the correction of the misconceptions will require a painful reduction of goals and
a still more painful deflation of egos. For to expand the
reality of independence at home many of the new countries
will first have to accept the narrowing of their illusory independence and importance on the world stage at large, even
as developing cleavages between the superpowers and some
of their respective major allies apparently generate new opportunities as well as awkward choices for Afro-Asians.

The struggles for succession in the eighteenth century were
dynastic ones. The key stakes were located in Europe for
the continental powers, overseas for England. The analogy
between the European wars of succession and today's critical succession has a facile side and a profounder aspect. It
is facile to recall that the issue between Europe and the
so-called Third World has been one of a twofold succession.
In the international arena, the apparently open succession
has been to Europe's leadership both as a seat of political
power and as a seat of moral thought and inspiration, pro-
testing the inhumane uses of that power. In the arena of
internal affairs, the role of the European colonizer as leader
and creator, if not as oppressor and exploiter, has also been
apparently vacated. The two successions have been readily
claimed by self-confident leaders of the less developed countries; the fact that most of these leaders were less ready to
honor the claim has long been obscured for the many (and
briefly even for the few) by the dexterity with which failings
in one area of succession have been matched by forensic displays in the other.

Even when and where revealed as hollow, the claims need not be forever forfeit. The claim to the succession in the domestic sphere, by far the more vital one for the undeveloped countries, corresponds to the imperative of an inescapable material task. But for the task to be taken up in earnest, the often onerous reciprocities in relations between at once independent and interdependent nations must be first accepted as a norm to be observed by political men rather than be protested as the neocolonial invasion of a fool's paradise. Even the claim to succession in the international arena may get another chance. But before this happens, the formulation of categorical imperatives of action for others will have to be based on a more austere performance at home and a less exuberant stance abroad.

The analogy has profounder domestic and international facets, however. In the domestic sphere, the eighteenth-century wars of succession were wars of nation-building in two respects, both relevant for the new states. The wars involved the adjustment of territories that would create economically viable units, notably in the case of Prussia; they stimulated developments in the science and practice of administration that would permit a centrally guided development of economic and human resources. A conspicuous example of attempted reforms was the underdeveloped, feudal great power in Europe's south—Austria. The more effective earlier efforts in the same direction accounted for the success of Prussia, and even Russia was enabled to intensify her participation in European contests. The ineptitudes in the war effort of France were traceable to a cause not unlike that of Britain's recent backsliding in economic competition. Colbertism had spent its momentum as an impetus to development and efficiency in France, while the partly derivative cameralism was ascendant in Central Europe. The country had to rest and the monarchy had to waste its credit before France could supply, in the nationality principle of the Revolution, the subjective element of nation-statehood.

The administrative revolutions were essential links in the progression from intrinsically personal unions held together by individual monarchs to institutionally integrated, so-called real unions, and in ethnically homogeneous states, to popularly cemented national unions. The liberal revolt against authority and the insurgence of nationality against alien empire in mid-nineteenth century Europe subsequently fostered the first wave of federative schemes for politically or ethnically fragmented areas in Germany, Italy, and in the Balkans. The projects did not materialize; the rebels against European colonial empires overseas were not the first to prefer integral sovereignties to the federative approach to political and economic fragmentation, wherever this was made possible or attractive by the outgoing imperial power. Outdoing the independent successors to Ottoman and Hapsburg dominions in Europe, many new postcolonial entities have gone all the way back to the organizing principle of the merely personal union. In the absence of meaningful nationhood, the personality of a charismatic leader-liberator has apparently been necessary to hold together too vigorously pluralistic and too vaguely or remotely historical units. Vindicated on the local plane, the principle of personal union appeared ready for use also on the regional plane, not least as a means of diverting attention from failures within the narrower frameworks of nation-building. In this respect, there has been no great difference between the ambitions of a king of divine right, such as Mohammed V of Morocco,

and those of divinized leaders, such as Nkrumah of Ghana
or Nasser of Egypt.

The formation of larger political groupings around provi-
dential individuals has seemed to offer an avenue of both
advance and escape. It might enable frustrated leaders to
rally the few indigenous technocrats and the many messia-
nists for an overdue state-building effort within an enlarged
territorial and economic frame. And while rendering possible
or unnecessary the adjustment of territorial and other disputes among neighbors, a viable regional grouping might
facilitate an escape from the ultimate futility of premature
forays into *Weltpolitik*.

Nation-building drew our attention to the efforts of the
enlightened despots of Prussia, Russia, and Austria; international activism recalls most of all the fortunes of Prussia. The
experiences of Brandenburg and, subsequently, Prussia were
those of many a flexibly aligned or non-aligned small state
in the dynastic politics of seventeenth- and eighteenth-century Europe; but Prussia learned her lesson and, after the
near-disastrous Seven Years' War, bided her time for a century until she re-emerged in the shape of Germany.

The lesson can be summed up in a few maxims. Once a
small, internationally active state sees the range of its profitable and relatively safe alternatives reduced, it can either try
to withdraw into a more passive policy or seek to strengthen
itself through intimate association with kindred states. The
small state will lose its flexibility when it seeks to exploit
differences between larger powers for so long a period and
in such a way as to make them feel conservative with respect
to the upstart, and no longer irreconcilable with respect to
one another. Such a development is precipitated when the
major powers come to realize one thing: that neither can

achieve a lasting advantage and commitment from the third, lesser states, and need not therefore seek to prevent an impossible advantage from accruing to the other great power. That is what happened in Europe by 1756; the golden age of the subsidized kings and princelings had come to an end. A like development, initiated exactly two hundred years later in Afro-Asia, has been terminating the golden age of the subsidized presidents and prime ministers as well.

Great Britain saved Frederick of Prussia from defeat and discredit at the hands of the reconciled conservative monarchies, the Bourbons of France and the Hapsburgs of Austria. Only the joint opposition of the relatively conservative powers of capitalist West and Communist East to the more dangerous upstart power, China, might finally save the less developed countries from bearing the main cost of a comparable reconciliation. Elements of a tacit alliance of the conservative powers against truculent China have already redounded to the occasional benefit of non-aligned lesser countries and leaders. But, insofar as the beneficiary of the emerging state of things, a Nehru of India, for instance, is forced to become a leader in peace or war who is beholden to one or both the superpowers, he loses more than he gains; no new fame can redeem the defeat of the preferred policy of free movement and mediation between the larger powers.

The statecraft of the Prussian and the statecraft of the Indian, incongruous as the parallel may be in many other respects, are two examples of one type of policy. India, like Prussia, can yet rise to an authentic role in the international relations of her time when she has sought and found nearer home the wherewithals of solid greatness. In this respect she differs from still newer and intrinsically small states which have sought prestige and profit in a game that even India

could not durably win. Their only chance of escaping ob-
scurity or worse is to gather new force in space, by more
or less freely accepted union with other states, and in depth,
by more or less persistently fostered development through
indigenous combinations of capitalist and socialist methods.
Only an altogether improbable dimension of success in these
efforts could halt the swing in the balance from being adverse to them in the foreseeable future, however. Under the
new balance in the making, the decreased capacity of the
new countries for movement and mediation will necessitate
a realistic adjustment in their international weight. By contrast, the increased material weight of the western half of
the reborn old Europe will inevitably increase her freedom
of action and will necessitate a realistic adjustment in her
international role.

CHAPTER II

The Conditions
of European Unity

Thus far, we have discussed the contemporary environment of unification efforts, rather than unity itself. In what follows we shift emphasis to the patterns of unity, beginning with Western Europe.

Europe has been loosely united twice since she emerged from the decay of the late Roman Empire as an identifiable geopolitical habitat of Western Christianity. The first unifier was the Church, with the Holy Roman Empire serving as a contender and a counterpoint. The second framework of unity was provided by the Concert of Europe, with the Holy Alliance as the contender for primacy. The span between the twelfth century and the nineteenth century witnessed the emergence of the nation-state, the articulation of Europe into a state system, and her political and economic expansion in the world at large. It witnessed also the rise of secular ideologies and the decline of religion as a norm, as well as instrument, of statecraft.

The main line of succession leads from the Church, as a political actor, and the Concert to the contemporary communities and councils. They all constitute the higher term in an essentially occidental dualism that is characterized by a fruitful tension between particular concepts or entities and transcendent ideas and institutions; and they are relatively free of attempts at premature syntheses of the ideal and the mundane. The parallel line of succession differs. It is characterized by exaggerations of Western or westernized ideals and models; it leads from the Germanic Holy Roman Empire to the Holy Alliance centered on the Third Rome, and from there to the Socialist Commonwealth of the Soviets. In their bids for presidency over a "united" Europe, both the Russian Tsar and the Communist rulers of Russia employed the dominant orthodoxy of the day for the purpose of advancing Russian power westward to the Atlantic, just as the Holy Roman Emperors had striven earlier to use the idea of imperial unity in order to penetrate toward the East and southward into Italy and toward the Mediterranean.

Our interest is in the occidental models and only indirectly in their Central and Eastern European competitors; and our interest in the occidental models is governed by the desire to identify some persistent factors that condition the process of unification among separate and largely self-dependent units of organization.

The Christian Commonwealth in Europe

Order through unity was an obsession with the infant heir to the chaos left behind by the Roman Empire, whose name was to be Europe. The aspiration for unity was the spiritual complement to the reality of narrow particularism which expressed the material needs of survival. As an unfolding reality, unity was hampered by the coexistence of several competitive foci of unity, both general and particular. Material conditions have since evolved toward favoring larger units of defense and welfare. The tension, however, between

competing principles of authority and organization has remained characteristic of European politics. This was the
case even at times when the principle of particularism seemed
to prevail in the supremacy of king or nation, and the general, transcendent principle seemed to shrink forever to
that of the balance of power.

At the peak of her global expansion Europe moved closest
toward breaking with her dualistic tradition and surrender-
ing herself to unadulterated interstate power-politics. The
secular-territorial state was old enough to be idolized and
not too old to be inefficacious. And the ultimately containing
role of the second term, in a dualistic order, was performed
by the global dimension of European politics; the world at
large served as an outlet for pent-up energies and as a
reservoir for countervailing power against hegemonic on-
slaughts on the continent. Self-destruction came quickly,
however, once the moderating potential that inhered in the
outside world began to wane and the outside world itself
began to close in upon Europe in the early decades of the
twentieth century. The material and moral decline of Europe
that culminated in the 1930's and 1940's was arrested only
when the loss of the global dimension began to be remedied
by the restoration of the second term in a dualistic order,
in the form of more or less supranational ideas and frameworks. No longer the dominant actor, Western Europe found
herself confined by superior powers and faced by the task
of developing appropriate new policies within her compass,
as well as with regard to the different kinds of outside forces
and powers. In this sense at least, the political evolution of
Western Europe has come full circle to her beginnings in the
continent's first so-called Dark Age; the unity which eluded
Europe in that age may still depend in our time on a more

successful exploitation of comparable circumstances and conditions.

Roughly twelve centuries ago, emerging Europe was in an inferior and even dependent position with respect to confining outside powers, the Byzantine and the Arab Moslem empires; and she stood in an ambiguous defensive-offensive relation with respect to the successive waves of still less developed pagan populations in Central and Eastern Europe. Rome was first severed and then alienated from Constantinople by diverse and yet interconnected events; among them were Arab pressure on Europe from the south and the east, the richer Byzantium's real or suspected policy of diverting invaders westward by means of subsidies, the Papacy's emancipation from Byzantium through alliance with the Frankish Monarchy of Charlemagne, and the doctrinal supremacy which the thus emancipated Popes claimed over the Eastern Church. The contest between the two branches of Christianity over doctrine, intensified by the contest over precedence in the religious conversion and political development of the populations in Central-Eastern Europe, insured that the West's confinement would be a protracted one. A fitfully expanding Islam eventually monopolized the confining function in the Christian East without meeting with effective Western opposition, even as the Crescent was giving way to the Cross in the extreme West.

Another characteristic common to early and contemporary Europe, in addition to confinement from the outside, is a pluralistic structure of authority within. At the beginning the overlapping spiritual and temporal authorities were limited in scope, attending mainly to the maintenance of order and justice; this tended to reduce frictions. At present overlaps occur and are advocated in order to enhance welfare for the parts and integration for the whole; the resulting government is expected to be at once big and just. Although big in the sum of governmental functions, authority is supposed to be just because restrained from above by the need for supranational consensus and from below by the new feudalism of organized group and provincial interests. Just as Western Europe as a whole reverted to the initial condition of confinement by apparently more forceful units of political organization, so did in a way the distinctive political creation of Western Europe, the sovereign territorial state.

In the Middle Ages the capacity for upholding security and justice in the face of omnipresent threats to survival was initially vested in the polar extremes. These were the infrapolitical local authority of the feudal lords and the imperfectly spiritual, suprapolitical universal authority of the Popes. It took time for the more comprehensive, but definitely circumscribed, secular authorities of the territorial state and of empire to supersede both of the polar extremes. The prefeudal Carolingian empire was strong enough to enter into an alliance with the Papacy; it was relatively strong because it was based on an authority that was delegated from the center rather than fragmented into practically independent local units. When the larger territorial units, the Holy Roman Empire and the incipient territorial states, were weak, their relationship to the encompassing spiritual-political authority was one that combined efforts at resistance to papal claims to supremacy with dependence on the Church and its clerics for technical assistance in administrative and social development.

The clericalization of the primitive state and the concurrent secularization of the dominant Church supplied an early example of a two-way colonial relationship. The dispenser of assistance grew demoralized as the material conditions of the party receiving assistance improved; and eventual separation by way of declericalization of the state posed problems not unlike those of decolonization. While it lasted, the symbiosis of Church and State promoted concurrent, if not even or uniform, political unification within larger and smaller compasses. It was not the last time that an initially harmonious relationship became turbulent as the smaller units sought to throw off dependence on the larger authority and unity; the relationship became relatively harmonious again when mutually emancipated and interdependent equals proceeded to re-establish something like an alliance between them. The interactive processes of unification in the period between the tenth and the thirteenth centuries—one under the encompassing authority of the Popes and another within the territorial and subsequently national states—have their twentieth-century parallels. One of these lies in the interaction between the American-led Western Alliance and the territorially and nationally defined little Europe; another is that between regional unifications in Western Europe and in the formerly colonial realm.

As a grand design, the Christian Commonwealth aimed at a special kind of equilibrium. The ideal was one of secular and ecclesiastical authorities functioning harmoniously in their respective domains under the supremacy of a Papacy which would, however, eschew direct political control; never realized, the ideal was perhaps nearest its realization in the twelfth century. The Church exercised most of the rudimentary welfare or social-service functions as well as a kind of suprapolitical authority. The Holy Roman Empire had lost its aura as a late embodiment of an idealized Roman Empire and fell prey to internal divisions; localism was declining; and the nation-state was not yet in the ascendancy. Supported by ecclesiastical courts, by episcopal organization, and by a network of monastic orders which were busy bringing into the fold even the long inadequately christianized rural areas, the Papacy reached its apogee as the supreme arbiter and upholder of peace among Christians and the defender of Christianity against its enemies.

Just before the onset of the twelfth century, a stroke of papal strategy, the First Crusade, seemed to bring unity to Christendom and exalt definitively the supremacy of the Popes. The situation was favorable. The confinement of Western Christianity from without continued as the Holy Roman Empire failed to expand decisively eastward, and the Moslems were sufficiently strong to press westward while being sufficiently divided to permit a successful Western initiative. The growing distress of the Eastern Church enabled Pope Urban II to organize a thrust that was offensive in character and defensive in objective. The position of Christendom was to be secured by two kinds of unity—unity in the West and a larger unity between the West and Christian East as an alternative to the continuation and aggravation of conflicts within and between the two branches of Christianity. The hegemony of the Popes in a universe so unified was to be insured by two convergent facts: papal leadership in inspiring and organizing the Crusade and the exclusion from it of potential competitive unifiers—the Holy Roman Emperor and the principal territorial kings. The Crusaders achieved the ostensible goal, the liberation of the Holy Places. But the larger and real papal objective of unity was frustrated, not least by the lingering animosities between Western and Eastern Christians. Conflicts among the Westerners themselves thwarted subsequently both the Holy Ro-

man Emperor's attempt to make the Second Crusade promote unity in the Empire and the French king's design to
replace the Pope as the head of unified Christendom in and
through a still later Crusade, in the fourteenth century.

The Crusades had, however, one lasting if limited effect
on unity in Europe. They imparted to the Western Christians
a sense of difference from the outlying world in the Near
East, a feeling which survived the decline of both popes and
emperors as the embodiments of the idea of unity. The feeling of a separate and valuable identity was undoubtedly for-
tified not only by provisional military successes but also by
the concurrent evolution of Europe as a viable economy.
Starting from a position of inferiority to both Byzantium
and the Moslem World, the West displayed over the years
a superior vital capacity for adopting, adapting, and spreading economic techniques and forms of organization. Increase
in arable land, the growth of cities, and the extension of lines
of communication by land and sea were the chief features of
expansion. The result was an economic surplus that could
sustain innovations in the domain of political organization,
enlarged in territorial scope and aiming beyond mere survival.

Once the Papacy had failed to give a lasting institutional expression to the unity of Christendom, it could
not but come into conflict with ever less co-ordinate
and ever more competing secular authorities. The conflict was not lessened by the tendency of the Popes
to affirm their supremacy more dogmatically as their ascendancy waned in reality. The decay was symbolized by the
diversion of the supreme tool of unity, the Crusades, into an
instrument of struggle within the European system. As a
last resort, the Popes attempted to meet the secular state

on its own terrain, notably in the Italian hothouse of incipient power-politics. This cost them in moral authority more than it could benefit either the papal states themselves or a possible material condition of unification: the establishment of a core-power around which might coalesce ever expanding unity. The Popes were not the last to discover the futility of linking a transcendent organization to a particular political and territorial status quo that would weaken antagonists and keep them disunited.

The gradual transfer of unification energies from the European framework of Christendom to the smaller territorial frameworks of states and nations disrupted the larger unity while it helped to identify more clearly the conditions of unification. The process that finally consolidated the congeries of feudal baronies into the territorial state covered the period between the thirteenth and the fifteenth centuries; it was long marked by conflicts between feudal lords and vassals, both within and between individual countries. These conflicts coincided on the whole with the expansion of judicial and tax-gathering functions of the central authority, with the expansion of the feudal monarch's core-holdings, and with developments in military technology favoring actors who disposed of superior material resources. Even at times when political unification was not progressing, the continuing economic expansion was sufficient to supply backing for the long-term unification process within enlarged territorial units, even if not within Europe as a whole.

The most arresting feature of the process lies, however, in the political sphere. The establishment of an elementary national authority and unity was easier in areas that previously had developed largely self-sufficient state-like local organizations under strong feudal authorities which were capable of maintaining social order and conducting orderly external warfare. The thorough feudalization of northern France and a similar state of affairs in England actually facilitated cohesion by reducing the need for irritating intervention by the emerging central power locally; the mutual frustration of underdeveloped provincial and central authorities elsewhere, especially in Germany, retarded national unification.

At least in one case, moreover, about a century after the First Crusade, national unification was advanced by a bold political thrust. The thrust of the French King Philip Augustus against his feudal vassal, the King of England, was characteristically a judicial one, on a sensitive issue of feudal ethics. The area to be unified was simultaneously confined by the defeat the French monarch inflicted on the external allies of unruly feudal barons. The combined strategic operation of thrust and confinement created the conditions for critical administrative reform and the constitution of France as a loose federation of provinces.

The shift of primacy from the Church and the Christian Commonwealth as a whole to the Monarchy and the national State as the main focus and framework of unity was consummated by the transfer of key loyalties. Both the rural masses and the rising middle classes wanted units of security and welfare larger than the village or the province; and the administrative elites, including eventually the ecclesiastical ones, were increasingly committed to the elaboration of frameworks that would be more manageable than had been the vaguely defined Christian society as a whole. The transfer, symbolized by the role of the great Cardinals in the unification and consolidation of England, Spain, and France in particular, showed how crucial was the earlier contest between Popes and secular rulers for effective control over transnational, ecclesiastic agents. The issue reappeared in contemporary international and supranational organization; so has the problem of the higher authority's capacity to penetrate through the intermediate authority, be it that of a great feudal lord or of a sovereign state, for purposes of appeal and redress.

Even a sketchy outline enables us to isolate key factors in a successful unification process. One such factor is an authority that is not contested, even if it is divided or shared. Medieval Europe as a unit lacked such an authority and suffered instead from contest between secular authorities, imperial and national, and the ecclesiastical authority. But perhaps more surprising, an effective authority must also be in existence within the component units to be unified. Such authority was present in the feudal components of France and England, and the two countries were the first to attain elementary unity and statehood in the West.

In a pluralistic structure, the problem of authority inevitably entails the related issue of hegemony or equilibrium. In medieval Europe it proved impossible to obtain either a lasting acceptance of papal hegemony or a working distribution of functions and powers that would implement the theoretically co-ordinate character of temporal and spiritual authorities in their respective spheres. The growing severity of the sanctions that one momentarily predominant authority tended to inflict upon the other bore witness to the absence of a tolerable institutional mechanism for reciprocal containment. Once authority was expressed primarily in terms of material power, the issue of equilibrium or hegemony became virtually insoluble and the interplay between a suprapolitical authority and several territorially circumscribed political authorities lost its potential for ordering and unifying the West. The waning second, higher term in the duality was to reappear only in the secularized idea of Europe and the Concert of Europe.

Another condition of the unification process appears to be the need for confinement of the unification universe. Such confinement was largely bestowed upon the Papacy by the hemming in of Western Christian Europe by powerful and intermittently antagonistic or even hostile outside forces. The confinement was gradually relaxed in the direction of the progressively christianized peoples in Eastern Europe and in the direction of the progressively weakened and temporarily even annexed Byzantium. The intensification of a single hostile threat—by Islam in the guise of the Ottomans —failed to offset this relaxation and thus to promote unity in Western Europe, especially when the Turk became an acceptable ally for Christian princes in function of hegemonic struggles in a politically disunited Europe.

Less favored than the Popes, the royal unifiers of the nation-state had to contrive confinement artificially from the outset. They did so by debarring insubordinate feudal lords and other dissidents from alliances with outside actors by means of military force supported by the invocation of successive principles of allegiance—fealty, loyalty to sovereign, and patriotism. The misuse of the guaranteed liberty of the German princes to enter into international alliances (provided they were not directed against the Emperor) was a key factor in delaying German unification until the late nineteenth century. The late seventeenth-century alliances of aristocratic French *frondeurs* with the Spanish national enemy in formally long unified France show the difficulty of upholding this particular condition of unification.

All these essentially political factors were reinforced by evolution in the domain of felt loyalties and in the means of fighting. Finally, economic expansion, which accompanied or was expected to follow the enlargement of the unit of organization, worked first for European unity and subsequently and more permanently for national unity, even if it was less self-consciously promoted and experienced by contemporaries than it has been more recently. In the domain of purposive human action, designs for ideal communities were more in evidence than deliberate strategies toward realizing these designs. The unifying thrusts of the Crusades and comparable acts by early feudal monarchs are only rudimentary instances of a unification strategy which can be more plausibly discerned in a less remote past.

The Concert of Europe

Submission to Peter was eventually to give place to the concert of peers as the ordering principle of the European comity. But before this happened, the middle period between the decline of the Christian Commonwealth and the rise of the Concert of Powers was occupied by violent tensions. The progressively secularized idea of Europe was strained to the breaking point by the temporarily reintensified religious character of European politics in the Reformation period. Only when the reassertion of particular, territorial and national, concerns had contained the religious antecedents of ideological conflicts while debasing them, could the institution of a concert begin to expand from its tentative beginnings in Renaissance Italy onto the European plane. As in the peninsula, a species of occasional concert was the

only transcendent institution that might impart some formal
unity to a system that otherwise depended on conflict and
particular alignments for the shaping of its unequal component parts and for bringing peripheral states and regions
into a single compass.

The test of a concert is in its ability to resolve or at least
mitigate two related kinds of conflict: the basic conflict implicit in the system of states itself and the specific conflicts
among individual members of the system. The intrinsic conflict is one between the assumption of a harmonious ordering
of unequal power which underlies the idea of the international system as a hierarchical order of greater and lesser
states, and the actual need for the balancing of competitive
power which underlies the principle and practice of the
balance of power. The concert can mitigate the intrinsic
conflict only insofar as it is effective in moderating particular conflicts, chiefly by facilitating a timely coalescence of
preponderant sentiment (more or less explicitly backed by
military power) regarding the opportunity of collective or
unilateral action. International politics can be regarded as
being ordered in an elementary way whenever elements of
concert coexist with competition short of actual war among
the great powers.

The three main modes of intercourse among major powers
—all-out war, competition, and concert—are related to one
another in a way that is not entirely haphazard. A formal
concert, best expressed in the institution of periodic con-
gresses, is almost always installed after a major war and
frequently tried before another such war. A less formally
implemented concert is typically associated with competition
short of war, especially when the competing powers come to
regard the transition from competition to war as unprofit-

able. The relation between concert and war is sufficiently different from that between concert and competition short of war to give rise to two distinguishable kinds of concert.

One is the formal concert that is most frequently initiated in order to implement a fundamental treaty or agreement among victorious powers. Membership in the formal institution has been traditionally reserved for major powers; the lesser ones have been reduced to occasional participation as a result of the principals calling in the minor parties or falling out among themselves. The most recent attempt at such a concert was made in the wake of World War II; the so-called democratic powers then drew self-consciously on the great exemplar of the aristocratic Concert of Europe in the period following the Napoleonic wars.

Under that system the great powers were the trustees of the European community, at least in constitutional theory. They were presumed to respect the rights and liberties of the lesser powers under the public law of Europe, and to seek agreement among themselves by way of timely consultation and serious negotiations in the highest European interest. This was, actually, the vital, if only implicit, commitment underlying the concert: the ruling great powers were to modify their drive for national aggrandizement by larger, European considerations as the condition of reaching agreement among themselves and securing the grudging consent of the lesser powers to their sway. The accord was, however, necessarily fragile, even when both conflicts and sanctions against the bested party were limited by the agency and by the conventions of the balance of power. The concert system engendered few if any radically novel arrangements for making the exercise of their limited obligations and expanded responsibilities truly mandatory for the major powers, while leaving them in possession of most of their rights to self-assertion. Despite occasionally effective resort to collective intervention, guarantee, and recognition of lesser states by greater ones, the Concert of Europe fell short of being an authoritative, equitable, and unifying international authority most of the time.

The concert was undermined by the inability of the great powers to reconcile the role of unifying authority with that of competitive actors lacking the necessary security and unchallenged status. Conflicts among the great powers deprived them of individual and collective prestige with respect to the lesser states; the shift in emphasis from collective authority to individual power and interests militated against self-restraint and judiciously exercised discretion which are vital for a paternalistic or oligarchical government that is to be responsible without being accountable. These weaknesses were not altogether unlike those of the earlier papal authority in Europe; and the concert system likewise suffered fatally when the particularistic principle of nationality and nationalism challenged the universal element implicit in any form of unity transcending the nation-state.

The innermost characteristic of the formal concert is pretense. The powers try elaborately to repress or ignore the conflicts among them by directing attention to major problems in third countries that might, in principle, be solved in such a way as to serve the interests of all concerned. The powers essay to govern and unite others while becoming increasingly unable to govern their own desires for unfettered action or outright aggrandizement. This kind of concert is either too much or too little; it follows too early after a war or comes too late to prevent another one. The powers are either too well cognizant of their respective power and interests if the concert follows upon a war, or too unsure of them, if it is convened to avert one after a long period of nominal peace. The formal concert is thus bound to fail, sooner rather than later. It seeks to reconcile too many contradictions: in structure, between equipoise and hierarchy of powers; in spirit, between too high an affirmation of harmony and a not sufficiently deep repression of conflict.

The other kind of concert is altogether different. Its natural place in time is the gray period of neither war nor peace; and it is characteristically informal and may even be tacit. It marks an emancipation of the powers from treaties and charters insofar as these inhibit their understanding and make them subservient to the claims and conflicts of third states. An informal concert is not normally meant to solve deep structural problems; it is designed merely to set limits to the contest surrounding these problems. The powers come to fear the consequences of unfettered action; and they become impatient with the attempts of smaller powers to govern by words the actions of the great.

The most flexible procedure is employed to identify and implement elements of concord; this is in accordance with the indeterminate nature of evolving power relationships among the major states at mid-point between major confrontations. The testing of will and the playing with fire that go on in peripheral and low-level conflicts create an ideal climate for the informal concert; they keep it from floundering into a premature option between formalizing the concert in yet another great-power directorate or dissolving it in yet another big war.

Whereas formal concert is keyed to a climax of wartime concord or warlike conflict, the informal concert is attuned to a transition. Its innermost characteristic is thus not so

much pretense as prudence; not impatience with major problems but patient nursing of structural transformations that
eventually dispose of problems by replacing them with
others.

An informal concert implemented the barest minimum
of the idea of Europe whenever the continent was not fend-
ing off one power's attempt to unify it by force or bending
under the ephemerally joint will of successful resisters to
hegemony. A long, if not continuous, spell of informal concert followed upon the failure of the post-Napoleonic formal
concert to safeguard the balance of power against both
France and the conservative powers of the Holy Alliance
without letting loose the forces of both social and national
revolutions. The Congress of Berlin in 1878 was, like the
earlier Congress of Vienna, made possible by a French defeat. But there the parallel ends. The rise of a strong unified
Germany in the center of Europe introduced an "honest
broker" between the divided principals of the one-time formal European concert: Britain and Russia. The locus of
profitable conflicts shifted to the peripheries of Europe; and
informal concert diplomacy sufficed most of the time to show
that no single power could reasonably hope to dominate the
inner and outer marches of the continent. This fact was
merely ratified in 1912–13 by the conspicuously successful,
if still relatively informal, great-power conference in London. The fact had to be reaffirmed with respect to Eastern
Europe, because it was there that the material underpinnings
of a competitive concert without war were already wearing
thinnest.

It is possible to idealize the concert while opposing it
as a more realistic peace-keeping device to more recent and
ambitious designs for regulating relations among states. To

do so, it suffices to stress consensus among the powers and affirm its existence in the past as the essential prerequisite of a successful concert. But no concert can rest primarily upon a political consensus, be it dynastic or ideological, just as a league of more or less united nations could not rest on a legalistic concept of justice. The element of consensus is to a large extent the refined product of existing conditions compelling co-operation, not a substitute for any one of them. Only residually is consensus an independent condition of a working concert; it stands last in line to account for what remains unexplained by the more material factors.

The same material conditions are necessary for both formal and informal concert. They differ from the conditions of more intimate unity and tend to be sufficient for any length of time only for the informal concert. To be sufficient for the more ambitious form of concert, the material conditions would indeed have to be matched by a wide-ranging independent consensus among the leading powers about the ways of governing an international system. Unfortunately, such a consensus can evolve only through the habits of society and condominium; it cannot precede these and nourish them for any length of time.

When describing the Victorian age, we have already touched upon the material conditions of a rudimentary concert. They can be grouped under the headings of shared deterrent, absorption, and outlet. The three are interdependent; to stress any one of them to the exclusion of the others is to risk confusing cause and effect.

The prime deterrent is that of all-out war being onerous to the point of being ruled out. In addition to the necessary but not always sufficient condition of equilibrium, the presumption against total war may rise from common material and moral exhaustion after a devastating war, such as the Thirty Years' War; from a shared sense of vulnerability to social-revolutionary terror, prevailing in the wake of the wars of the French Revolution and Empire; or from the terror of yet untried new weapons, such as the nuclear ones. The stimulus to concert that arises out of the deterrent is weakened when one power can credibly pretend to fear the breakdown of the deterrent less than do others. This is most likely to occur when an internationally revolutionary (that is, expansionist) power is also a socially revolutionary one or when a conservative power finds itself in a social-revolutionary situation. The concert of the Victorian age broke down when leading men in Russia (and to a lesser extent in Austria-Hungary) came to regard successful war in support of a half-heartedly resumed imperial drive in Europe as the only way to contain internal ferment. A working concert for our time will become possible when the social-revolutionary temper of Soviet Russia has been muted, if only in contrast to that of the more recently revolutionary power in Asia, and when Russia's expansionism in Europe has been manifestly checked by an enlarged, twentieth-century equivalent of unified Germany to the west of her.

The prospects for a concert are good when, being deterred from provoking war, the powers are absorbed in internal concerns. Deterrence and absorption are closely linked; one may cause or at least accentuate the other. The post-Napoleonic concert in Europe was partly induced and temporarily held together by the desire of ruling elites to concentrate on controlling social-revolutionary forces in their respective countries. The concert tended to break up when the uneven spread of these forces outgrew the ability of the powers to agree on a joint response to social and national upheavals.

This failure to agree became virtually unavoidable once the very magnitude of the rising forces inhibited the Eastern powers from devoting themselves to feasible internal reforms, which had been rendered or revealed necessary by the preceding war, and led them instead into repressive policies at home and abroad. Conditions appeared to change for the better later in the nineteenth century. Industrial developments in the major countries intensified internal social problems while rendering them intrinsically soluble, a combination of factors that is most likely to deflect governments from hazardous policies abroad. The material base of the informal concert was gravely compromised, however, when Germany, caught between the headstart of the British and the initial industrializing spurt of Russia, could begin to doubt her ability to collect in peace the political dividends of her industrial growth.

If Germany's absorption in internal pursuits tapered off too quickly and came to an end prematurely, Russia's did not have the time to take root and both modernize and stabilize the decayed order. The Germans calculated that the growth of Russian material resources, including the military ones, would be too rapid; the Russian decision-makers acted on the assumption that it would be too slow. Neither of the two ruling elites felt able to rely on domestic developments for insuring stability at home and an expanding role abroad. The resulting climate was favorable to a fateful convergence of anticipations about the comparative growth of national potentials in the long run and comparative speed of military mobilizations in the short run. The preoccupation with economic growth in the 1960's has been more self-conscious than ever before; the formally declared economic race is now between the United States and Soviet

Russia, with mainland China in Russia's earlier position of an underdeveloped giant trying to rush up from behind.

An economic growth-race will tend to absorb and stabilize; politico-military activities at the peripheries of the international system will likewise distract actors and only superficially unstabilize the system. They constitute an outlet, which is the third of the main material preconditions of concert. Even when peripheral activities have been prompted originally by an equipoise of power at the center of the international system, they help transform the frustrating feeling of deadlock into a quickening sense of mobile equilibrium. Major powers henceforth have other things to do than to feel or act alarmed at the slightest shift in the relationship of ready forces at the center; they incline instead to act on the assumption that there is an approximate balance in organic factors of power. Even more than some of the early Crusades, the colonial wars and recent "neo-colonial" activities have helped to alleviate confrontations among states unable to stand still and unwilling both to wage war on each other and to contemplate a federative response to the threat of mutual conflict. The quest for compensations and the barter of advantages, diversionary movements, and a loosening of alliances through marginal diplomatic infidelities can go far enough to relieve hostilities at the center, even if they stop short of disrupting centrally vital ties.

The greater is economic or military activity in peripheral areas of contest, the greater is the need, moreover, for diplomatic activity at the center. Along with arms-races and war-substitutes such as colonial skirmishes and economic-aid competition, diplomatic activities supply an outlet for the socially and psychologically requisite display of competition among powers which have found themselves in a stance of rivalry within an interdependent and dynamic system. Really explosive pressures decline in the system without the powers ceasing to be on the alert; the contest remains within the limits that have been set by a common distaste for stepping it up and that are permitted by the cultivation of sufficient capability to accept the escalation of the conflict in the future. The result is tacit agreement to delay the decisive showdown and see in the meantime whether it might not be avoided altogether among the powers as then constituted. Such an agreement is the essence of the so-called consensus allegedly underlying a concert.

Always precarious, the concert is threatened whenever the forces and factors that make it possible turn against it. One such deformation can occur when the deterrent breaks down, because the conditions making war undesirable for all no longer exist, or an actor seeks release from too many partial setbacks or too long sustained tensions in a decisive test of strength. Another deformation is exuberance from extraordinary domestic growth, which makes continued absorption in domestic affairs apparently unnecessary, or frustration over internal failures, which makes such absorption apparently impossible. And still another perversion is the return upon the system of the activities that have been previously channeled through outlets. The unavoidable frictions among adversaries come to be exploited by war parties within countries, and crucial alliances re-emphasize solidarity so as to compensate for infidelities in peripheral areas or activities. Such developments are all the more likely because they conform to the tendency of old peace settlements to erode and to be finally disrupted by hard-to-assimilate new forces.

The peace settlements that emerged from the wars of

Napoleon and from World War I fell victim to erosion, more suddenly in the second case than in the first. The order emerging from World War II is still in the process of being defined; our period resembles, however, the nineteenth century in the place assumed by the rise of new forces rather than by the reassertion of old drives in modified forms, as was the case between the two world wars. The difference is that these new forces have now managed to come into possession of state power in a large segment of the state system. This has ruled out the purely repressive approach to them. But the fact that the revolutionary forces have been reduced to operating within the context of relatively stabilized interstate relations has increased the possibility of controlling and finally absorbing them by traditional means of statecraft.

The process will be slow and tortuous when the revolutionary new force is in control of one powerful territorial state; the operation is likely to be even more delicate, but the process may be speeded up if such states are two or more and are faced by a similar number of comparably strong non-revolutionary powers. At the time of Charlemagne and later, the Christian West found it easier to come to terms with Islam when two competing Caliphates confronted two discordant segments of Christianity. At a later stage of religious conflicts, the cause of toleration was ultimately enhanced by the fact that a four-cornered contest pitted Catholic France against the Catholic Hapsburg powers and aggravated the conflicts of interest between expansionist Protestant Sweden and the Protestant princes within and outside the Holy Roman Empire. In the instance of a secular ideology, the integration of nationalistic France into Europe was finally eased, for both liberal England and autocratic Russia, by the national unification of Germany. A specific political ideology may constitute a deeper identity between two states than does religion; and opposition to such an ideology may bind other powers more closely together than opposition to aggressive nationalism. But it may well prove to be easier to absorb Soviet Russia in a meaningful, if informal, concert once there is a really strong Communist China, and the two revolutionary powers are faced by a united Western Europe as well as by the United States of America. Polarization is more difficult to maintain as occasional cross-alignments take place in function of compelling state needs and take the doctrinal sting out of the competition.

The conditions of a working concert tell us more about the circumstances under which a united Western Europe might participate in a reconstituted formal or informal global concert than about the conditions under which the states of Europe might begin the reconstruction by uniting. To avoid war is not the same as to unite in peace, although the desire to break the vicious circle of conflicts may precipitate unity in favorable circumstances. The impulse to avoid war among member parties might thus be the one condition which concert and union have in common, unless the shared condition be that of equilibrium or accepted hegemony, which conduce to ruling out war and are the alternative conditions of both concert and unity.

There may be some difference between concert and unity even with respect to war, however. It could be argued that reluctance to resort to war between parties susceptible to uniting is not so much a particular condition of unity as it is a general premise underlying the strategy of unification among sovereign states. In any event, the response to the reluctance to drift into conflict will vary depending on whether the system is confined or wide open with outlets and escapes from competition within it. The existence or deliberate promotion of confinement, singled out as a condition of unity in medieval Europe, is most sharply at variance with the existence or deliberate search for outlets, identified as a condition of concert. Another difference is that between the condition of absorption in internal, mainly economic, concerns and the anticipation or actuality of economic expansion through unity. All these differences stand for the difference between two forms of co-operation, one of which is more positive and, if based on more than coercion by superior force, can be expected to be more enduring than a mere concert.

The State and Unity in Modern Europe

The unification of Germany and the prospective unification of Western Europe, we have already noted, can be compared with regard to their immediate effect on world policy in the two eras. We shall now see that the internal dynamics of the two unification processes are also comparable. To show how, I shall draw on the already outlined material and conceptual conditions of unification among independent units of political organization. They fit the unification process as it unfolded in Germany and has been unfolding in Western Europe in two distinct phases—the liberal-constitutional phase and the conservative, strategy-oriented one. First to be discussed are the *material conditions of unity: authority, hegemony, political confinement, and economic expansion.*

There are good psychological and political reasons for

the significance of authority as one of the material requirements of unification. Responsible directors of a sovereign
state will be reluctant to let the history of the state as an
independent entity end on a note of failure, to be remedied
by merger. Moreover, the existence of an effective authority
within the component units will tend to enhance the initial
efficacy and gradual extension of new central institutions.
When embarking upon unity schemes, therefore, national
authorities must be manifestly capable of maintaining political stability in the member countries-to-be and of insuring
their economic viability. Just as two or more neurotic partners are unlikely to constitute a healthy union, so two or
more internally unsettled states are not likely to constitute
a stable community.

The liberal, parliamentary workers for German unity are
identified with the revolutionary year 1848 and with the
National Assembly deliberating in the free city of Frankfurt.
Their effort to exploit the collapse of traditional authority
within the German states failed over the unwillingness of the
monarchs, and notably the Prussian one, to erect a new
structure on the collapse of the old. The moment of hope
that the King of Prussia might accept the so-called National
Constitution and his election to the Imperial dignity was
definitively shattered by the renewal of revolutionary unrest
in the spring of 1849. Dynastic authority had first to be restored, especially in Prussia, independently of representative
bodies and even against them, before unity could again become serious politics, transcending the German state system
while building upon it.

The conditions of internal authority in the states of
Western Europe roughly one hundred years later were comparable. The problem was acute in France and to a lesser

extent in Italy, latent elsewhere on the continent. The first postwar unification attempts coincided with instability in the political order, threatened by the Communist party, and with derangement in the institutional balance between executive and representative organs. In the political sphere as well as in the economic one, a basic question was raised: can a larger unity be wrested from joint admission of the failures and inadequacies of the nation-states; or must unity flow instead from the merger of new and positive elements of strength, separately if co-ordinately set into motion?

In the economic realm, the first thesis, identified with Jean Monnet, was contradicted by the insistence on prior national recovery of men like Pierre Mendès-France. Charles de Gaulle merely applied the second thesis to the political and military realms. He nonetheless shocked thereby the politically liberal economic nationalists and the doctrinaire supranationalists into something like an alliance for the defense of the Republic, the European Communities, and, incidentally, NATO. The ensuing constitutional struggle in France has had points in common with the contest between Bismarck and the parliamentary forces in the early 1860's.

The parallels can be extended to the economic aspect of stability, economic viability. The political upheavals of 1848 were preceded in Germany by agricultural and commercial recession, producing social discontent. The 1850's and 1860's saw rapid economic growth. Similarly, the economic competence of the Western European states was more firmly established in the late 1950's than it had been a decade earlier or, for all that, at the time of the Briand project for a United States of Europe in 1930. Germany's unification was preceded by substantial industrial expansion. Europe's economic unification followed closely upon a differently timed and phased, but basically comparable, economic revival in the individual member countries. In both instances, existing authorities were anything but inhibited by their proven capacity to assure the economic viability of their countries on the eve of momentous changes.

The requirement of effective authority bears on conditions within countries. It is matched by the requirement of an acceptable distribution of power and authority among them. The issue here is between satisfactory equilibrium and tolerated hegemony by one partner.

The liberal-constitutional phase of unification in both Germany and Western Europe witnessed an attempt to dissolve the problem of national power and hegemony in an institutional equilibrium of checks and balances. The counterparts of the draft constitution of Frankfurt were the draft treaties instituting supranational communities for Western European defense and a political superstructure.

The need in the first case was to check and balance Prussia until she stopped wanting to be Germany and became German; the later problem was to check and balance a Germany relieved of Prussia perhaps only temporarily, at least until she became reliably and permanently European. In both instances artificial equilibration may have been impossible from the very beginning. West Germany was no less difficult to counterweight within a little Europe with no more than an outside guarantee by the English-speaking nations than Prussia had been within a little Germany without the aid of the German-speaking elites of Austria. The German princes, dragooned into the so-called Erfurt Union by popular pressures, readily abandoned the attempt as soon as they recovered control of their governments and of the traditional counterpoise to Prussia, the German Confederation including Austria. On the later occasion, the task of equilibrating was abandoned no less readily by the French National Assembly when it turned against the European Defense Community and chose instead the more traditionally structured Western European Union which included the British counterpoise, once the French government was in a position to liberate itself from military pressures in Southeast Asia and to spurn openly its major ally's diplomatic persuasions.

The situation was different in the second, conservative phase of unification. By 1870, Prussia's hegemony was assured by the victory over Austria and by the annexation of both the territories and the votes of a number of Austria's German allies in the new North German Confederation. If anywhere, the safeguards for the South German states participating in the proclamation of the German Empire in 1871 had to be sought in retained elements of sovereignty and in the links of a social contract forged in the joint military effort against France. In the comparable phase of Western European unification, West Germany has been growing stronger and gaining weight within the North Atlantic Alliance relative to the 1950's. But France too has meanwhile come to feel strong enough to rely on an informally plebiscited Franco-German alliance for appeasing apprehensions, and on national performance in the economic, political, and nuclear-military realms to offset West Germany's no longer so superior potential. The change of attitude may not be a permanent one. But for the moment, the Fifth Republic has infused with political self-assurance the economic gains that had originated under the Fourth. It has dared to experiment with alternatives to its predecessor's addiction to constitutional formulas and international guarantees—such as the not fully observed British commitment to keep a specified number of divisions on the continent during the lifetime of the European defense arrangements permitting German rearmament.

The issue of hegemony declines in importance as the problem of internal authority appears to be on the way to solution. A nation's self-confidence is reflected in its trust in the operation of a larger equilibrium than can ever be secured contractually. Whereas in the past France assiduously solicited Great Britain as a weight against Germany in Western Europe, she has now ventured to keep Britain out of Europe and let others seek her out as a weight against a Franco-German hegemony. De Gaulle's apparent intention to keep Britain out altogether, at least for the time being, brings up the third and probably most important condition of unification, political confinement.

The issue raised by the condition of confinement is that of necessity as against freedom, just as in regard to the preceding conditions the issues were those of health as against neurosis and of equilibrium as against dominance. The fragment of the state system to be unified must first be confined. The regional system can be confined from the outside, through pressures that emanate from the larger system, or by deliberate efforts from within to eliminate alternatives to unity. The public has a role in confining the range of options from within whenever it sets barriers to alternative alliances and configurations. Nationalism or regional supranationalism, expressed in antagonisms and favoritisms, most commonly erects such barriers without being their only source.

With regard to the condition of confinement, the first phases of unification again compare unfavorably with the later phases. In 1848, as in the years following 1948, there was a tendency for political forces to overflow the area of possible unification. The would-be unifiers of 1848 reached too far out, both north in the direction of Denmark (for Schleswig-Holstein) and south in the direction of Austria, encouraged by the vacuum of authority consequent on revolutionary upheavals in both the German and the non-German parts of Europe. The final decision to exclude the German parts of Austria from the new federal state was made meaningless by the concurrent reassertion of counterrevolutionary forces. The confining pressure, when it came in the form of repressive counterattack of autocracy (symbolized by the intervention of Russia in Hungary), was too strong and found the German political universe too divided to be manageable. In the comparable phase in Western Europe, the Soviet pressure was made manageable by American backing; it was thus a factor for integration. But complete dependence on outside support, institutionalized in the Organization for European Economic Co-operation, in NATO, and in the Anglo-American guarantees linked to the European Defense Community project, ruled out a sufficient political confinement of the unification universe from the West.

In the 1860's, by contrast, the German unification universe was confined by Prussia's contest with Austria and, subsequently, by her contest with France. The political exclusion of Austria was prepared in the field of economics, effected militarily, and consummated diplomatically. To begin with, Bismarck prevented Austria from a closer association with the Customs Union centered on Prussia, the *Zollverein,* which Austria had long wished to absorb in a vaster Central-European trade zone centered about herself. The *Zollverein* adopted a liberalized trade policy just before 1866 and was tightened institutionally even before 1870; thus vitalized, it helped keep even pro-Austrian northern and southern German states within the orbit of Prussia, while Bismarck proceeded to exclude Austria by military defeat in the first round and kept her excluded from the unification game in the second.

In the critical year of 1870, a Prusso-Russian accord had raised the threat of Russia's involvement on the side of Prussia should Austria expand the conflict on the side of France. Together with early Prussian military successes, this sufficed to deter Austria-Hungary from attempting to carry the South German states with her into a belligerent alliance with France and thus cleave open the confinement effected by Bismarck's diplomacy. Bismarck had already pressured the South German states into a secret defensive-offensive alliance against France; and Napoleon III co-operated unwittingly with Bismarck's strategy when he entertained the idea of seeking territorial compensations for Prussian gains in the north at the expense of France's traditional clients and allies in South Germany. The national feeling that already inhibited the diplomatic flexibility of Austria-Hungary was sufficiently aroused to counterbalance even in Bavaria and Württemberg the dislike for unification on Prussian terms. The diplomatic confinement of the system was thus complemented by an internal barrier to distracting alternative alignments with the key outside power.

In the early 1960's, de Gaulle has been engaged in excluding the so-called Anglo-Saxon powers from the European unification process, much as Bismarck excluded first Austria and subsequently France from the German unification process. The stabilization of mutual nuclear deterrence between the United States and the Soviet Union has favored the strategy by exposing Western Europe to new dangers and requiring the West to revise its concepts of joint defense and political organization. The United States has assumed a stance with respect to Western Europe reminiscent of the attitude of France toward German unification. The sentimental concern of Napoleon III was for nationality in all Europe; America's has been for supranationality in the European part of the West. Both France and the United States, as the major Western wing powers of the day, favored in principle the unification, by consent, of a strong central power to serve as a dependable factor in a new balance of power and as an ally against the Eastern colossus. In the decisive phase, however, both well-wishers inclined to make their sympathy for unity conditional on tangible guarantees of the new entity's future political conduct and of their own continued preponderance in the military sphere. German unity had to be made finally against France and possibly could not have been made with her support; Western European unity may yet feed on more or less hidden political opposition by the United States to particular expressions of unity in Europe after overt American support for its approved forms has failed to bring unity about in the preceding phase.

From the viewpoint of an indigenous strategy, the role of the United States is a limited one. It is to prevent Soviet Russia from interfering with the European unification process, while ceasing itself to offer distracting trans-Atlantic alternatives to closer intra-European alignment. As long as Britain, the other former guarantor against Germany, does not separate herself from the United States, she too has to be excluded—at first from the European Economic Community. The EEC has found itself in the position of the *Zollverein*. It has been called upon to evolve far enough to withstand the attraction of a British-sponsored economic association and contain the reactions of the continental states to disliked aspects of de Gaulle's unification strategy, even while being still reversible enough to make a mobile political strategy at all feasible and plausible. Complementing the bond of economic interests, a European spirit has been expected to hinder the small states from resisting French leadership on the continent by appeals to the American leadership in the Atlantic West.

Measures to impede political forces from overflowing outside the universe that is presently susceptible to political unification have coincided with a critical development in Western Europe. Much as deficiencies in national authority increase the importance of the issue of hegemony or equilibrium, lack of political confinement magnifies the importance of economic expansion as the driving force behind political unification. But great and certain as they may be, economic prospects or realizations will not suffice unless political and military factors are channeled so as to support economic enticements.

The manifest advantages accruing from the Customs Union to the German states for several decades before unification were not sufficient to advance the German states beyond diplomatic confederation and the loosest possible military organization. In the period between the Austrian and the French wars, both Bismarck and his political ally, the National Liberal Party, failed in their attempts to use the popularly elected all-German Customs Parliament to promote political, along with economic, unity in South as well as in North Germany. The expansion of production and consumption within Western Europe, while she was undergoing the pangs and reaping the benefits of withdrawal from her expansion overseas, may have preceded or merely coincided with the movement toward economic unity. An increase in prosperity has nonetheless been established as a credible impetus to unity for Western Europe and for comparable regions elsewhere. Welfare in common has followed upon proven viability individually. It remains to be seen whether economic integration in Western Europe can be secured against the pressure of conflicting agricultural and other economic interests by political and military forms of unity, or will remain isolated and hence recede.

The outcome depends greatly on the interplay of the material conditions with the *conceptual prerequisites of unity: design and strategy.* In order to bring the material conditions of unification into focus, the conceptual ones have had to be kept in the background. The separation has been artificial, since concepts participate in forming conditions even in the preparatory phase of unification. But the separation is also practically significant. Once the principal material conditions are roughly realized, they become less important than the dynamic components of design and strategy, which would achieve little in a refractory material environment. Art without matter is futile; matter without art, inert.

The design comprises the institutions of unity to be realized. It must be both original, in the sense of being adapted to the unique character of the community to be established, and realistic, in the sense of fitting the perennial conditions of successful political construction. Unlike the design which is concerned with new forms, strategy is concerned primarily with the ways and means of moving from established forms to alternative ones. Whereas the design must be original, the strategy is more likely to be effective if it employs proven means of statecraft even toward innovating goals. The design could also be called constitution, in the broadest sense of the term; strategy must, therefore, be something other than the convening of constitutional conventions and mobilizing of domestic support for implementing a design. Design is more important when decisive actors are committed to unification as self-evidently beneficial for all members; strategy is the key factor when actors are committed to the pursuit of national goals and to unification only insofar as it is the best means to attain them. Accordingly, while the motive force behind design will commonly be conviction and persuasion, the driving force behind strategy is necessity, which works through the compulsion of all actors by unfolding events and of some actors by other actors. Having constitutional connotations, design is more typically associated with motives and models found in domestic experience; strategy entails a more definite foreign-policy orientation.

In the first phase, the unifiers in both Germany and Western Europe worked chiefly through a design. In 1848–49 the design was that of a federal constitution based on common nationality, universal suffrage, and unified administration, topped by an all-German Emperor. Not for the last time, a constitutional and political transformation was to be accomplished on a plane transcending the states that had withstood it internally. The ambitious constitutional project failed and Austria followed the failure with a series of reform plans. These reserved greater roles to individual states and were alternately resisted or radicalized by Prussia as part of one more contest over leadership in a unification universe.

The design of the 1950's was not federative in its guiding principle. It called for functional communities integrated by the progressive implementation of the supranational prin-

ciple in executive and representative organs. The architects
of the design were committed to unification, and sought unification by persuasion and consent. Their motives were to
be found largely, though not only, in the internal domestic
sphere; the desire to revive decadent French capitalism was
matched by the desire to safeguard West Germany against
the revival of potentially resurgent militarism and extrem-
ism. For its models, the design could refer back to the vision
of nation-states gradually integrated on a broad front encompassing economy, army, and a progressively constitu-
tionalized political authority. The economic core of the design, the Coal and Steel Community, was both a recollection
of and a reaction against the institution of prewar cartels,
originating within individual countries and spreading into
the international domain, if not directly into the foreign-
policy domain. All considered, the design has been both
more original and more realistic than was either the constitutional plan for German unity in 1849 or the Briand plan
of 1930. It has, therefore, been provisionally more successful in the economic sphere.

   Throughout, from the treaty establishing the European
Coal and Steel Community to the Treaty of Rome setting up
the European Economic Community, the unifiers pursued
their objectives by parliamentary action, by popularizing
propaganda, and by solicitation of supporting pressure from
abroad. There was bargaining between individual governments to be sure; but this took place within the existing environment that was to be changed only by the implemented
design rather than being worked upon by a foreign-policy
strategy in such a way as to precipitate the design's realization. If the merit of the design-makers of 1848 was to prepare spirits, the design-makers and partial implementers of

the 1950's have created, in addition, the habits of co-operation. Both, it may be said in fairness, demonstrated in the process the limits of their method.

The question before Europeans now is whether the approach by way of design can generate ever expanding unification. Integration in particular sectors—such as coal and steel and international payments—led to the common-market approach of the European Economic Community. But the degree to which the different functions and activities are autonomous has so far inhibited the spilling over of integration from economics into the political and military realms. The sluggishness of the integrative dynamic when limited to economics is not disposed of by the tendency of Eurocrats to describe economic integration as essentially political, in view of the expanded role of the modern state in economics.

The progress toward joint military and political institutions was arrested with the defeat of the projects for a European Defense Community and a European Political Community. Several years after a new start, it has remained uncertain whether the progress could be resumed from the enlarged base of the Economic Community. It might be possible, as has been suggested, to reform and merge the executive organs of the different communities and to expand the assembly. With its standing thus enhanced, the executive might become an incipient federal cabinet; and the expansion of both the powers and the popular base of the representative organ might make it into an incipient federal parliament. Such institutional development might, in ideal conditions, further increase the integrative potential of the European decision-making process, which is already characterized by problem-oriented exchanges between supranational technocrats, national ministers, civil servants, and parliamentarians. The over-all result would be a transfer of primary loyalty by a growing number of people from the country of their origin to the larger European community at one extreme and to particular provinces and regions at the other.

Such prospects are far from certain however; they may be countered by the following propositions. Conditions in Europe are no longer revolutionary, and unification of hitherto independent units is not an evolutionary process. In order to move beyond the uneven accomplishments of the European communities and of the community-oriented Europeans, a traditional foreign-policy thrust has become as necessary in Western Europe as it was in Germany. The sovereignty of the reconstituted state may have to be again exalted before its hard core can be reduced by the very means of its final affirmation. Only actions guided by a strategic concept are appropriate for this purpose.

A particular strategy of unification has been broadly identified in the earlier discussion of the medieval unification process. It may now be defined in relation to modern European politics. The strategy consists of two movements, corresponding to two phases. In the first phase, a concentrated thrust at a key point initiates a movement toward disintegration in the existing structures, or it at least raises the prospect of such a movement. In the second phase, the danger that disintegration will actually occur or spread tends to induce a reintegrative movement, as states rally to contain and absorb the unacceptable consequences of such a development. The actor employing the strategy aims to compel potential partners to rally around him by bringing into the open available alternatives; such compulsion is different from coercion that would dispense with demonstration. The strategist seeks to show that his country's position is at least as strong as that of others, and to show further that the segment of the state system that is to be unified cannot continue as before.* Alternatively, an actor may set out to demonstrate his outright superiority and the inability of other states to continue in the old pattern without escaping coercion by the stronger state. The first variant of the strategy is compulsory but not hegemonic; the second is both, with regard to potential partners. The outside powers must be encouraged to refrain from interference; to this end, they must be given reason to believe that the new unit will be internally stable and that it will abstain from unstabilizing foreign policies.

If action of this kind is to transcend tactics and become strategy, it must satisfy two main criteria. First, the action must reach out of the compass of day-to-day affairs as regards both the stakes and the planning. The directing authority must be ready to deploy major resources and to stake its survival on the outcome. While planning, the strategist must anticipate both the immediate responses to the first disintegrative thrust and the length of the time-span that is likely to be available for the eventual reintegrative movement. And he must take into account the repercussions of the initial thrust in space, both in the inner zone which encompasses the prospective parties to unity, and in the outer zone of merely interested or affected powers. Second, while transcending ordinary stakes and planning, the strategist must stay within one field of action when according means with objectives. If the objectives lie in the foreign-policy

* A variant of this strategy may be a demonstration of weakness, not so much to future partners as to current domestic opponents. The British government failed to shake the EEC by setting up the Free Trade Association and was compelled to inflect its strategy in this direction.

domain, the principal means must also be found there, and similarly for the domestic arena. A strong tactical bias will mark an action that is deficient in stakes or in the scope of prevision, and devious in shifting its means and ends freely between the realm of international politics and that of internal politics.

Bismarck acted, and de Gaulle may be regarded as acting, in ways that fit such a definition of strategy and that contrast with design as well as tactics. Whereas Bismarck was a Prussia-firster, the prime commitment of de Gaulle has been to France. For both men a larger unity was a valid goal insofar as it secured the essential interest of their country: aggrandizement for Prussia, grandeur in equality for France. The commitment to unity need not be less efficacious for being conditional. For both conservative statesmen the means and ends of strategy lay in the realm of foreign policy. The main strategic thrust occurred in the narrow military field, and it was as forceful as the preceding ground-clearing measures had been devious.

Bismarck's final thrust was at the neuralgic point of French political and military opposition. The Prussian committed the full military strength of his country and staked his own person on the rightness of his calculation, as he had done before against Austria. The calculation bore on the sufficiency of resources available to achieve the immediate objective which was the military success of Prussia; and it bore on the attainment of success in a time sufficiently brief to preclude outside intervention and the escape of hesitant allies from the compulsion. The lesser German states were compelled to rally lastingly and organically around Prussia, as the sole alternative to the disintegration of the German state system being followed upon by overt Prussian coercion.

The disintegrative thrust against Austria was followed by partially forcible reintegration in North Germany; the potentially disintegrative second thrust against France precipitated a unification of all Germany that was neither fully spontaneous nor altogether involuntary.

Bismarck demonstrated the superiority of Prussia over rival powers, Austria and France, and consequently, the desuetude of the old confederal pattern. His strategy was both compulsory and hegemonic; de Gaulle's strategy, to the extent that it can be rationalized, has been at the most only compulsory. The first step and immediate object have been the acquisition of a military capability that would establish the value of France as ally for the major nuclear powers and her material equality with a Germany that may be potentially stronger than France, but lacks nuclear weapons for the time being. The calculation behind the French thrust at the neuralgic point of the Atlantic coalition has focused on two vital issues. One is the sufficiency of France's material resources to achieve the immediate objective which is the development of a striking force that would be capable of punitive retaliation in the last resort; another is the possibility of attaining the capability in the course of an international *détente* sufficiently long to allow a first phase of incipient disintegration in the Atlantic and the West European frameworks to be followed by a second, reintegrative phase. In the latter phase, the Western European states might have no other recourse but to rally to France's concept of European defense and unity, in order to escape unacceptable alternative prospects.

What such a prospect or prospects would be cannot be foretold with certainty. They may encompass, without being exhausted by, debilitating political and military hegemony by the United States, disruptive competition between again fearful France and again feared Germany over privileged alignment with the United States or preclusive alignment with the Soviet Union, and divisive intrigue and nuclear blackmail or coercion by the Soviets. The demonstration of danger and resulting necessity can be expected to unfold gradually in the apparently available long time-span. But a critical point is likely to be reached sooner or later. If not before, such a critical moment might come with the establishment of a diplomatically creditable and militarily usable French striking force, with the initial moves of West Germany toward a nuclear capability outside a politically constraining framework, and with growing pressures on other Western European states to acquire the henceforth essential attribute of statehood in a meaningful fashion. Developments of this kind would confront Western Europe with a tangible, rather than a merely hypothetical, threat of material overexertion and political disintegration into uncoordinated, mutually endangering, military and political policies. In a politically sufficiently confined and economically integrated universe, political and military unity might then be the only positive response available to the interested countries within the range of their traditional and contemporary foreign-policy options. The nature of such options and their capacity for converging in some kind of regional association are, next to the global setting, key factors for judging the prospects of an initially disintegrative strategy.

What Kind of Europe?

De Gaulle's approach to European politics can be questioned on many grounds. Our immediate concern is with aspects of the Europe coming into being, her constituent spirit, scope, and structure.

The creation of Bismarck has never lived down the master-builder's phrase about blood and iron. His achievement has since been condemned as unnecessary, on the unprovable assumption that German unification in peace, freedom, and stability was inevitable, or at least highly probable, in any event. The achievement has, moreover, been indicted as harmful, on the proposition that Bismarck single-handedly introduced ruthless realism into Europe and rabid nationalism into Central-Eastern Europe at a time when the first had been superseded by the liberal world-view and the latter was only a potentiality. It can be argued, however, that Bismarck's strategy of unification was only an early and conspicuous instance of the world-wide passing of the brief and ambiguous liberal experiment in foreign policy, just as the strategies of de Gaulle have not caused the end of the foreign politics of bipolarity in Europe, following upon its demise in the world outside Europe, but have merely called attention to it. Both Bismarck and de Gaulle rank as the outstanding practitioners of traditional statecraft in their time; but neither was the only one to practice the art any more than he is likely to be the last.

It is true that the creation of Bismarck was a conservative one, both in its conception and its subsequent development and exploitation. It was supported by the socially conservative rural masses and gentry, and by the self-consciously realist captains of an expanding German industry. German intellectuals and professional people criticized Bismarck's methods both before achievement justified the means and after ultimate failure at least temporarily condemned both means and achievements in their eyes. The position of de Gaulle in the spectrum of supporting and adverse social

forces has been comparable to Bismarck's; so has been his
place on the spectrum of available forms of statecraft—notwithstanding specific differences in political method and in
the appreciation of the political significance of economics.
Bismarck's avowed model for mobilizing rural and urban
masses as a force behind authoritarian, but socially fairly
enlightened, policies was Napoleon III. Recourse to popular plebiscite, or referendum, in testing and demonstrating
mass support may be the main feature common to the
Second Empire and the Fifth Republic in internal and
European politics.

Even an essentially critical re-examination of Bismarck's
work must take into account the real alternatives to it. Had
unity been achieved without or against Bismarck, it would
probably have been won by the externally expansionist liberal nationalists. And if unity had not been achieved, latent
forces of instability might well have come to the surface in
response to the growing tension between the scale of economic potentialities and acute social problems in Germany
and the scale of her parochial political organization.

Similarly, the autocratic methods of de Gaulle's diplomacy have to be judged in a larger perspective. The alternative to a "nationalistic" Europe may be a progressively disunited Europe or a united Europe of the Eurocrats unable
to generate the heightened sense of distinct individuality
that alone can give meaning to practical co-operation, offset particular nationalisms, and restrain regional and group
conflicts. All states involved in the European unification
process differ from contemporary Soviet Russia by having,
in national frameworks, successively and lastingly exhausted
both the drive and the capacity for continental hegemony.
The formal self-assertiveness of French European diplo-

macy is the lingering expression of past weakness, not the harbinger of France's third drive for European hegemony in three hundred years. An identical, and in part similarly inspired, misassessment of the resources and ambitions of France in Europe was made after World War I; it had disastrous consequences.

Totalitarian methods in internal politics have, for the time being, receded along with the capacity for hegemony; hegemonial expansionism and totalitarianism may be indeed but two facets of the same surge to power. The typical European society is now a pluralistic one, with a tendency toward a stable and authoritative government. The trend seems to be away both from parliamentary anarchy and from authoritarian dictatorships; both extremes seem to have reached, or be reaching, the point when they did all they were able to do for national unity and economic growth. European dictatorships originated in conflicts among hereditary enemies, in resentments against outside dictation, and in overburdening of central institutions by unfamiliar tasks. To the extent that these determinants are still potentially valid, a European union of states, even under the auspices of a de Gaulle, might be least likely to promote dictatorships. This has not, of course, been the view of those who have regarded the British counterpoise to a potentially hegemonic and almost certainly internally unstable France or Franco-German combination as a necessary safeguard for internal freedoms as well as interstate liberties in Western Europe.

Britain's participation in the Common Market and in the process of political unification, while affecting the spirit, concerns directly the scope of European unity. Ever since the early 1940's, de Gaulle has been rehearsing updated vari-

ants of the three main options that have been available to
French foreign policy for two and a half centuries. The
oldest option is an offensive or defensive alliance with the
strongest available Eastern European power or powers of
the moment; it was to permit a vigorous policy toward the
strongest or most aggressive of the Germanic powers in the
middle of the continent. Another option is an alliance with
the Anglo-Saxon island power or powers in the West; this
connection has traditionally legitimized a weak French government and both reinforced and restrained it in foreign
affairs. The third option is a stabilizing alliance of a self-
confident but non-expansionist French government with the
conservative Germanic power in the center of Europe. Two
centuries ago this last option was realized in opposition to
Britain and Prussia; the first threatened the position of France
as a first-rate global power, the rise of the second threatened
the territorial integrity of the principal German power, Austria. The unification of Germany in 1870 threw France back
into a position of insecurity, reminiscent of the earlier Hapsburg encirclement. It reduced French alignment alternatives
on major European issues to a Western alliance with one
or both of the Anglo-Saxon powers, or an Eastern-European
alliance. The emphasis has tended to shift to the Western
option whenever the French capacity to act independently
has declined. De Gaulle has revived the German option,
briefly and platonically at the end of the war, and more
seriously after his return to power, in order to strengthen
France in her dealings with the meanwhile enlarged wing
powers. In this respect the foreign policy of de Gaulle has
been that of Louis XV and Vergennes rather than that of
Richelieu and Louis XIV.

  To include Britain in the alliance with Germany would

constitute an innovation. The arrangement would probably suffer from the disadvantages of all triangular relationships. Moreover, it might very well compromise the utility of the German alliance for France with regard to both the United States and the Soviet Union, as well as the utility of the French alliance for Germany with regard to the Soviets. While the Germans could retain the illusion of a choice between the French and the Anglo-Americans, France has been under a real pressure to choose between West Germany and Britain and to define the scope of a united Western Europe in such a way as to exclude Britain at least provisionally. France might see leadership in the European community pass to Britain and through Britain stay with the United States, should Britain be brought in before the European hierarchy and the European-American relationship were crystallized. The complementary economic interest has been to reduce Britain's competition within the Common Market, as long as protective tariff walls are sufficiently high to reorder trade to the advantage of the founding members, and to eschew revisions of agricultural policies that might further curtail the precious elements of identity in French and German rural interests.

Britain's own position has been weakened politically as well as economically. She is now incapable of implementing at least two of *her* traditional ways of relating herself to the continent. She is no longer sufficiently strong in her home base and in her overseas resources to act as the leader of a grand coalition against the only possible present source of military challenge in Europe, Soviet Russia. And she has not been sufficiently free of external pressures to inspire a peacetime Concert of Europe, and lead it while leaning on a strong conservative continental state. A reduced capacity

for leadership has focused attention on Britain's third way of
relating herself to the continent, which is the negative facet
of the first two: that of keeping continental Europe from
undertaking joint action and organization without Britain's
controlling participation. It is yet to be fully accepted that,
for the divisive policy, Britain lost not so much the capacity
as the rationale—along with world empire and traditional
means of defense—without acquiring a valid new one in the
field of economics and trade.

One of the extremely rare occasions when the continental
nations came close to acting in unison contributed to Britain's losing America for the first time, in the War of Independence. The reluctance of the British to lose the United
States for the second time and definitively has impelled them
since World War II to hedge about their adhesion to European unity. Whatever may have been the real motives and
intentions of the British, a succession of their proposals and,
still more, counterproposals in the domain of European
integration has appeared suspect when viewed from the
continent. The French had the support of the doctrinaire
Europeans when, for instance, they fought against the British plan to associate the Common Market with a British-
sponsored free trade association by way of the Organization
for European Economic Co-operation in 1958, just as they
had the sympathy of the Eurocrats when they bargained
hard over the British application to join the Common Market
in 1962. The British have been suspected throughout of
the desire to dilute through association what they were unable to extinguish by non-co-operation. The risk for Europe
is that Britain's divisive form of relationship with the continent would continue to predominate even within a mod-
ernized fusion of the coalition and concert approaches.

Both risks and suspicions grow when Britain acts as if, on the one hand, she still could implement the grand-alliance and concert options in the enlarged Atlantic framework by invisibly guiding America's foreign policy and, on the other hand, as if she could not hold on to any real role even within reduced Europe without bodily leaning on the United States. Britain is likely to commit herself fully to Europe only when she has assimilated the painful truth that she no longer has any special role to play in either of the basic perspectives that survive and vie for primacy in American foreign policy. Britain is not needed any more as the naval guarantor of America's isolationist-imperialist policy that concentrates on the Western Hemisphere and the Pacific. And she is no longer the strategically *or* sentimentally sufficient reason for the Atlantic policy of intervention in and for the European balance of power. Her role in the world policy of the United States— as the helpmate now rather than the amiable rival—can be henceforth better performed from a strong and autonomous European base than from the nominal center of increasingly unreal overseas relationships. In these circumstances, the last great act of their special relationship to America might well be for the British to help the upcoming political generation in the United States to implement *its* confused ambition of seeing the country act as a culturally and ethnically neutral world power that has outgrown both Europe-centered internationalism and Europe-rejecting isolationism.

When denying, in January, 1963, the application of Great Britain to join the Common Market as both belated and premature, de Gaulle acted, therefore, on considerations that were only in part peculiar to him. Neither he nor France have thereby necessarily embraced the Central and Eastern European options as against the Western and specifically

British connection for all time to come. When Britain has taken full measure of the alternatives to the west of her, she too may be ready to draw closer again to France and either supplement a Franco-German alliance that was meanwhile consolidated or take the place of a vacillating or headstrong West Germany. Should this happen, de Gaulle will have undone the supreme efforts of Churchill to graft England on the United States and to redeem thereby the frustration of Chatham's American conquests by de Grasse. A tolerable defeat for both erstwhile contenders over overseas American possessions would take its place alongside the ultimately suicidal frustration of both French and German power by Britain on the European continent. The struggles of old-regime Europe would finally be over, clearing the way for a new European beginning.

Whereas Britain blocked drives for European unity in the past as a condition of world empire, and Germany sought to conquer Europe for the same purpose, most Frenchmen were interested in world power only or mainly as a remedy to the metropole's being blocked, isolated, or subdued in Europe. After the rise of Germany, Britain and France were driven into alliance in Europe despite their continuing rivalries in the world at large; at least since the Suez crisis, the position has tended to be reversed. Paris and London have been separated on European issues while discovering new affinities in the domain of decolonization and postcolonial construction. The new challenges may yet help associate Britain, the traditional world power, with France, the primarily European and Mediterranean power, in a new world policy for Western Europe.

The unification process in Europe has now reached the point when exploration of alternative alignments and conditional exclusions has become possible and even desirable. It has been possible because the framework is still sufficiently elementary to permit recasting; and it has been desirable if the institutional structure is to be rooted in more concrete foreign-policy orientations and commitments than is the commitment to a "united Europe within the Atlantic community." Not only enthusiasm for disarmament or arms control but also impatience for unity among sovereign states may be usefully tempered by concern for an acceptable political and territorial settlement. This is true especially if these sovereign states have traditional differences of outlook and yet uncrystallized attitudes toward problems arising out of their just-experienced diminution and just-beginning revival. In the aftermath of the war, the loss of faith in past orientations and a feeling of inability to evolve valid new ones on a national or even a collective basis made out of European unity an apparently self-sufficient program. It became tempting to act as if the void of concrete political purpose could be filled by the elaboration of institutions and of only marginally political functions; as if the diversity of individual expectations could begin to be reconciled only after the achievement of formal unity.

De Gaulle has reversed the trend by stressing substantive purposes with respect to the military defense of Western Europe, the political relations among prospective members of a European union, and the relations between Western Europe and the outside world. But his approach gives rise to two legitimate questions. Can the approach bring about European unity? And, has de Gaulle been actually committed to meaningful unity? The questions must first be met with a counterquestion regarding the kind of unity one is speaking of. Regardless of the spirit and the scope of united Western Europe, what is to be her institutional structure?

There is one kind of unity that is of primary significance for the external relations of states. This is the unity among sovereign states that creates a new actor for the purposes of foreign policy and military strategy. Such an actor comes into being when the component states have committed themselves to the formulation of a joint will and have equipped themselves with the means to formulate and implement this will separately from other powers. These are the minimum requirements; degrees of integration are of importance in such a view only insofar as they are demonstrably necessary to insure prompt and efficacious external action.

The integration of Germany continued after the country's far from integral unification in 1871. But the German unification process ceased to be of absorbing interest to international relations when other powers in West or East could no longer play on regional separatisms in Germany with significant success. Western Europe will be unified when the Western Europeans have acquired the means of acting in common on the great issues of defense and diplomacy and have developed a reliable reluctance to identify national interests with the interests of extra-European powers at the expense of the continent's internal unity and international standing. Just as political confinement is a key condition of unification, it is an irreducible feature of existing, if loose, unity. It comes to mean the disappearance of the right as well as the inclination to seek with outside powers redress for grievances against partners. A recourse to alignment with outsiders would be tantamount to denouncing effective membership in the union. The ultimate right to secession is unavoidably maintained in a loose union; but its practical effect is reduced when the ensuing economic dislocations and political reprisals constitute a graver deprivation than the one originally suffered.

A relatively loose union in Western Europe may be politically necessary as well as sufficient for some time to come. Unity in Western Europe depends on events in the East, just as the extension of independence and unity eastward depends on policies in the West. The great unknown which militates against a premature definition of the institutional structure of Europe is the evolution of relations between the Soviet Union and China and among members of the European Soviet bloc. The time for making a serious beginning toward unification is now, though the maturing of Western European unification may be usefully retarded. It will take time to identify with something like certainty the first principal role of a united Western Europe. She may have to serve primarily as a counterpoise to a reconsolidated Sino-Soviet bloc, along with the United States; or else she may be called upon to act as a pressure from the West on the Soviet Union, thus matching that of Communist China from the East, so that she might serve eventually as an alternative for Russia to a rebellious China. In order to perform either of the two roles, Western European unity must be efficacious; but at the same time the Western European structure must be sufficiently independent and flexible to facilitate the rearrangements that would be necessary to fit Soviet Russia and the Central-Eastern European states into a single European system.

Quite apart from any romantic attachment to the nation-state and realistic skepticism about new institutional designs, uncertainties of this kind would suffice to relegate the final form of unity to the category of secondary considera-

tions. The design of the institutions for a united Germany
was of no special importance in the thinking of Bismarck;
the same has been true for de Gaulle in the European setting.
Both men favored confederal patterns to begin with, giving
preponderant weight to the institution of councils to the
detriment of joint executives responsible to representative
elected bodies. Their principal, immediate interest lay in
those arrangements for a joint military policy and command
over the partly autonomous military forces of member-states
that would facilitate a vigorous foreign policy. Even before
the North German Confederation was supplanted by the
more closely federal German Empire, however, Bismarck
was prepared to borrow from the book of his opponents. He
instituted universal suffrage, albeit without real authority
for the representative organ in any but economic questions
that could not seriously interfere with military preparedness.
Similarly, de Gaulle has adopted the idea of popular participation in the making of Europe, although through a
referendum rather than through periodic elections for an
authoritative common assembly. He has also come to tol-
erate supranational commissions and authorities, although
with controlled powers. Like Bismarck in the period between unification in North Germany and unification of all
Germany, he may yet find it difficult or impossible to wield
the adopted devices in such a way as to make them promote
his view of political unity.

The constitutional design has no other function for the
foreign-policy strategist than to institutionalize the provisional results of the strategy that engendered unity as one
of its products. The governing criterion is that the design
neither submerge the original entity, Prussia or France, nor
preclude the evolution of the new structure. Once in the

saddle, Germany would learn to ride, was the belief of Bismarck. The corresponding belief of de Gaulle would be that only when Western Europe has come within sight of a joint and separate nuclear capability will she both need and develop the required political authority for operating the military command and control structure.

Yet the most resourceful statesman is not in full command of the forces he has set in motion or with which he has allied himself. Bismarck adopted the idea of German national unity, which corresponded to the contemporary needs of Germany, as gradually as he rather suddenly brought the unity about. De Gaulle's more gradualist strategy may bring about circumstances requiring a sudden commitment to previously undesired forms of European unity. A true statesman will not risk being bypassed by events and thus to jeopardize even the originally sought, limited objective.

De Gaulle may have gone too far in downgrading the institutional advance already achieved and in slighting, in favor of the particular, the universal or supranational level in the dualistic relationship typical of European politics at its best. His action has had all the virtues but also the shortcomings of cautiously innovating conservatism. The tentativeness of de Gaulle's approach to the forms and even the principle of Western European unity has been the strength of his open-ended strategy as regards Europe as a whole. The turmoil which de Gaulle will have caused before Western Europe is united may well make it easier for Europe to be effective if and when unity is accomplished, either by de Gaulle or others. But a reluctance or inability to do more than indicate trends and constellations for the future and to consolidate the provisional results of the strategy in organs for co-ordinating policies might last too long, compromising Western Europe's unity and France's international position. It may be the lot, but it cannot be the purpose, of the heroic statesman to obtain for successors, as the reward of compromise or capitulation, what he himself failed to secure by the right of an accomplished conception.

The final question is whether the strategy of unification, as we have defined it and attributed it to de Gaulle, can produce unity. The fact that it worked in Germany suggests that it can work again. However, the attitudes of outside actors were by and large favorable to German unification, and the relationship of forces within and outside the German lands was even more auspicious for Bismarck's strategy. It remains to be seen whether the European unification process can fare equally well in a changed and enlarged, but in some respects still comparable, setting.

There are times when an outside power can directly support the unity or a desired form of unity of other states. The time may now have passed for the United States to determine the scope and structure of Western European unity, just as it did in the 1860's for Russia in arbitrating German unity between Prussia and Austria. But the United States has retained the ability to do, or refuse to do, what Russia did in 1870: use its power and influence in such a way as to promote the unification potential in a foreign-policy strategy. This may mean at the present juncture for the United States to abandon Britain and its other European protégés to their European destiny without abandoning Western Europe to the Soviets, and, having thus contributed to the confinement of the European unification process, to support and thus shape the nuclear effort of France as an instrument for unity rather than obstruct it as a factor of disintegration.

Among the lesser states looking to the United States, Italy holds a key position. She can act as the greatest of the European smaller states or, once again, as a great power by the consent or convenience of the more truly major powers. Italy's international alignments, including her first major alliance with Imperial Germany and Austria-Hungary, were motivated by considerations of internal politics and interests more than those of any other major European state. The foreign-policy motives of Italy's alignments were primarily those of prestige and aggrandizement to be derived from differences between other powers and between France and the German powers in particular. This inclination alone would have justified keeping Italy out of a Franco-German alliance before it was firmed up; this exclusion was liable to injure the sense of prestige of an Italian government sufficiently to predispose it to the idea of an alternative alignment with the United States, with the encouragement of diversely motivated domestic interests. The combination of French economic pressure and of popular opposition in Italy to an exclusive alignment with the German powers eased Italy out of the Triple Alliance before World War I; comparable pressures might similarly affect a contemporary triplice associating Italy with the United States and Britain, should this prove necessary for reminding Italy of the primacy of her continental ties in contemporary conditions.

The key to the fate and shape of unity in Western Europe lies, however, with West Germany more than with Italy or the still lesser states of Western Europe. The key to the German attitude itself can be found more reliably in the basic givens of the German predicament than in the personalities of individual chancellors. West Germany will long depend on the military protection and guarantee of the

United States against the Soviet Union and will give it high priority, as long as the military and specifically nuclear protection provides security against all conceivable inroads as well as scope for continuing military and political rehabilitation of the country. But any democratic government in West Germany will have likewise compelling reasons to secure itself against French *revanche* diplomacy as well as to assure itself of French political and moral backing. West Germany has no ready substitute for France; only France can legitimize the German interest in reunification and in politically and otherwise unprovocative military rehabilitation in the eyes of the less forgiving smaller nations of Western and Central-Eastern Europe. She has, moreover, no apparent substitute for a strong France. Only such a France can combine diplomatic firmness with diplomatic flexibility in regard to the Soviet Union; the firmness is guaranteed and the flexibility is circumscribed by France's own need for West Germany if she is to have the respect of the Eastern as well as the Western superpower. The United States can threaten to give up France for West Germany in Western Europe; but Germany cannot desire the isolation of France if she is to avoid being herself isolated one day on the European continent. France has a real, acceptable alternative to West Germany in Britain in the West and in the Soviet Union in the East; both of these French alternatives entail a diminution of prospects for German reunification. West Germany's long-term alternative to France is extremely dangerous for her. It will continue to lie in the East as long as the United States cannot offer Germany a dynamic policy against the Soviets without turning both parts of Europe against her; and as long as no West German government can indefinitely go on buying domestic tolerance for political stalemate or worse with increases of economic power and military prestige in and through association with the United States, Great Britain, or both.

Despite the fact that West Germany has inherited the capacity of the two German Reichs of modern times to inspire apprehensions regarding her future behavior, her actual position has resembled so far that of Imperial Austria as the enfeebled German power in the center of Europe. As such, she can serve as the continental ally of the English-speaking island nation, enter into a conservative alliance with France, or throw herself into adventures in Eastern Europe. The first option used to be the most frustrating for Vienna when it came to recovering lost territory (Silesia, from Prussia) and is apt to be such for Bonn. When this conclusion has been reached in Bonn, Washington may well hesitate to make West Germany choose between the Anglo-American alliance and the French one. The discovery might, however, come too late to avert the consequences of disunity and to permit the exploitation of existing opportunities for unity.

A United States that becomes a controversial and partisan actor in the politics of European unity steps upon a historic ground haunted by failure. The lot of medieval Papacy is not too far-fetched a precedent on the strictly secular plane. The United States, too, embodied at the outset of its contemporary European career the idea of the West and of supranational unity for Western Europe. It was the source of legitimizing approval for the resurgent political powers and provided essential support for economic and political reconstruction. As the only effective authority in the system, moreover, the United States was not only the accepted leader against outside dangers but also the peacemaker and equili-

brator among the West European states and nations seeking
new political identities and frameworks. The projects of the
European Defense Community and the related European
Political Community marked the climax of the American
role and the beginning of its decline.

With the opportunity for the institutional consolidation
of American leadership in Western Europe now lost, too
intimate an involvement by the United States has threatened
to be disintegrative. As old, indigenous centers of power
have revived in Western Europe, the idea of the West has
been subjected to more than one interpretation. The idea
has been inevitably territorialized in the process, in the sense
of being conditioned by the particular interests of the different territorial states. The United States has become, as far
as Europe and her unity are concerned, one power among
other if lesser powers, reluctant to be content with merely
setting the stage and leaving the Europeans in control of
at least one drama of the age. No longer able to legitimize
other political actors by extending its blessing to particular
policies and attitudes, the United States has been reduced
to practicing a secular form of excommunication—from
the fold of true believers in and workers for European and
Western unity. And unable as well as unwilling to unify
and expand the sway of the West by leading a crusade
against the East, the United States has been driven, like the
Popes before, toward conducting divisive crusades against
political opponents within the West.

Misused authority is a wasting asset, likely to be such in
the future as it was in the past. Moreover, by setting itself
against a particular indigenous strategy for European unity,
the United States has run the danger of defeating an initiative at the cost of creating a legend. The legend, regardless

of actual facts and intentions, would be one of American opposition to European unity. An indictment of this kind dogged more rightly than wrongly the role of the Popes in Italy, the traditional role of France vis-à-vis Germany, and, up to a point, Britain's role in Europe. But it took little factual justification to make the Germans blame all the European great powers for their own inability to unite in mid-nineteenth century.

The American attitude toward Europe has been a composite of the attitudes of the European powers toward German unity at the earlier juncture. Like Britain in the case of Germany, the United States has favored the rise of a liberal new power in the center of the system; like Russia in the earlier case, it has favored a power that would be a bar to revolutionary upheavals within and outside; and like France under Napoleon III if not before, it has favored one that would give tangible guarantees of continued responsiveness to the sponsor's interests and security needs. Again like Britain, the United States has jeopardized its position by fluctuating between levels of active interest in European unification politics. It has acted like Russia, when alternately favoring, or appearing to favor, one or another potential unifier and when directing or being swayed by the lesser client states within the unification universe. And it has behaved like the French Emperor when favoring European unity as an idea, but opposing it both as a process undertaken under any but American auspices and as a force that would constitute anything but a dependable and dependent ally.

The positions of the European powers on the issue of German unity were determined largely by their conflicting expectations as to the impact of the unified country on extraneous questions. Prominent among these were Russia's drive to the Straits and her exposed position in Poland. Similarly, the American attitude to European unity has been swayed by extraneous concerns. One concern has been for a military balance of power and deterrence against Soviet Russia; military and political independence for Western Europe might jeopardize the existing balance. Another preoccupation has been with the possibility of agreeing with the Soviet Union on a nuclear test ban and a more comprehensive arms control; prospects in this area might be doomed and achieved progress nullified by nuclear diffusion. And still another desire has been to dispose eventually of the enlarged Polish Question of the day, the issues of partitioned Germany and occupied Central-Eastern Europe; uncontrolled developments in Europe might lead to either of the undesired extremes—violent explosion, or real or apparent composition by European actors only.

The United States is not alone in its apprehensions. The price of unity for some in the currency of stability and welfare may be too high for others. Is it likely to be exorbitant in the European case? The query about the kind of Europe to unite leads to questions about the world at large.

CHAPTER III

A United Europe
in a Divided World

In order to be settled positively, the issue of German unity had to be approached as a European problem. The point has been reached when unity for Europe is inseparable from the global problems of defense, diplomacy, and development in the years to come.

Western Europe and the Defense of the West

While American opposition to independent nuclear deterrents was for a long time argued mainly in military terms, the issue is primarily a political one among the allies. This fact might facilitate an eventual accord, but it conceals meanwhile a danger. A political conflict can escalate with more ease than a military confrontation; and in a nuclear age interallied politics is the first to become again conventional and unlimited.

Still, the military aspect cannot be ignored. Regardless of whether the United States is in a position to assist Europeans in the development of a nuclear force at this juncture, the motive force to be harnessed before European political integration is now a nuclear force. The United States can, however, be expected to look with favor or even with equanimity upon the development of a national or a joint European deterrent force only if it can be convinced of the validity of certain propositions. These propositions are the following: that an independent European force would not necessarily interfere with the defense of the United States and the West, and might even contribute to it at a later stage; that there is no practical alternative that is militarily less problematic and politically safer; and that a Western Europe, united around a separate common deterrent, can be expected to be a factor for stability in the coming world politics of increased flexibility or of intensified conflict.

The key military questions in the trans-Atlantic debate have concerned the effect of a virtual American monopoly in strategic nuclear forces on the defense of Western Europe; the effect of independent nuclear capabilities in the hands of the Europeans or of the French on the defense of the West; and the effect that expenditures on nuclear arms might have on a greater European effort in the field of conventional forces, as well as the effect an increased conventional capability might have on the defense of Western Europe and of the West.

Attitudes have had more in common than viewpoints. European critics of American nuclear policies and American critics of French policies have shared one fear: that the other side might have enough capability to create additional dangers and cause greater destruction than necessary, but not enough to assure effective defense. On both the nuclear and the conventional-armaments questions, confusion has muddied the psychologically vital distinction between the ally's capacity to act effectively and his willingness to act when it hurts. The Europeans have wavered between questioning the will or the capacity of the Americans to defend Western Europe by nuclear arms. They have feared, on the one hand, that the will might be undermined by the concurrent growth of Soviet nuclear forces and of a conventional alternative to nuclear defense, and, on the other hand, that the capacity might be diminished by the diversion of United States capabilities to the defense of positions nearer home, such as Cuba. In either case, the Soviets would be in a position to blackmail Europe. The Americans, for their part, have seemed unable or unwilling to distinguish clearly between the will and the capacity of the European governments to step up expenditures for conventional forces under alternative formulas for nuclear defense, and to distinguish, further, between their economic and their political capacity to do so. Will grows out of capacity, at least in part; but while capacity can be usefully discussed among allies, a strategic concept that raises in too acute a form the question of an ally's determination to act in peace or in the face of war cannot but erode an alliance.

Finally, both sides have sought support for their preferences in conflicting hypotheses about the likely reaction of the Soviet adversary to a European nuclear force or an increased conventional force. Responsible Americans have feared that a European nuclear capacity would be harmful for both the United States and Europe if it were capable of triggering Soviet nuclear forces against the United States. A Soviet attack might then be a pre-emptive one, on the main arsenal of the alliance, or else a retaliatory one, against vulnerable population centers in the United States in reprisal for the countercity targeting of a weak European force. Either contingency might derange American dispositions for implementing the commitment to Western Europe. For their part, Europeans have tended to feel that the United States failed to understand either its own real motives or the defense interests of the West. The American government need not fear the trigger effect of a European force if it was actually prepared to go to the assistance of Western Europe in all circumstances. Even if the need for co-ordinating two Western nuclear forces created new complications, these would be more than offset by a great new advantage. A decentralized Western deterrent would reduce the danger of a Soviet miscalculation, based on an opportunistic assessment of the relatively simple relationship between only two nuclear opponents.

A weak European capability *might* initially permit only strikes against cities and invite retaliation in kind, possibly extended beyond the Atlantic. But, the Europeans could argue, the United States strategy of selective strikes against military targets only (the so-called counterforce strategy) has bred comparable dangers for *them*. The strategy depended on a second-strike capability vastly superior to the capability of the Soviets. Such a superiority will be either impossible to maintain indefinitely or, if it existed at the moment of conflict, would drive the Soviets into a desperate strategy of nuclear terror. The cities hit most or held as hostages would, however, be European cities. They are sufficiently close to the Soviet Union to be reached with even a diminished capability, and sufficiently remote from the United States to discourage American retaliation in kind as an alternative to accepting the termination of the conflict in a draw.

The intensity of the trans-Atlantic debate has reflected a double anxiety. The European fear of Soviet counterdeterrence has been matched by the apprehensions in the United

States for the American-controlled counterforce strategy. Washington's apprehensions have been as exaggerated as the parallel ones of the Europeans, if it feared only that a European capability might increase the common danger (by striking prematurely rather than in the last resort to trigger a reluctant American ally) and reduce the efficacy of inter-allied defense (by striking the wrong targets, or striking cities while the United States was trying to adhere to a selective counterforce strategy). It can be argued, instead, that even an inferior national or European nuclear capability could usefully supplement the superior American capability.

Several contingencies can be envisaged. A European nuclear force might serve only when the United States force did not go into action on behalf of Western Europe, and it would serve then only as a last resort or for bargaining over the terms of non-resistance. The opposite, and allegedly only possible, case is that of the United States' capability being activated. The European capability could then be meshed into the American force by way of prior allocation of targets; or it could be kept in reserve just as would be, under the counterforce theory, the unused remainder of the American capability, for bargaining and deterrent-retaliatory purposes. Ideally, the European capability should be protected physically in hardened sites or by means of dispersion. But a weak, unprotected force might actually be immunized by being placed near population centers and thus exempted from a Soviet counterforce strike, still assuming that it is possible to implement the counterforce strategy. In order to obtain the greatest possible flexibility in use the European force would not have to be integrated and should not be integrated with the American nuclear force.

As nuclear forces become more dispersed and better protected, the span of time available for interallied consultation and co-ordination increases again. The range of formulas for co-ordinating actual employment is likely to remain bounded by two extremes. One basic formula is for committing both partners in Western defense to joint action; such action might, as just suggested, entail the conditional inaction of the European deterrent. The other formula would permit each partner to undertake separate action; but even a separate action is not truly independent, because it profits by the adversary being obliged to reserve a capability against temporarily inactive powers and because it can always be fused into joint action by triggering the opponent into a response encompassing the passive party as well. The second command-control formula—for separate if not independent action—can hardly be applied to individual countries within the narrow geographic compass of Western Europe; this difficulty is a decisive factor for European unification in the foreseeable future.

A somewhat revised formula, intermediate between complete separation or complete integration, might become conceivable as the European force grew. Such a force might be made capable of joint action with those United States' strategic forces only that are based in Europe and assigned specifically and conspicuously to NATO-in-Europe at the time of crisis. The time for such an association would come when the European nuclear force had generated sufficient political unity in Europe to facilitate decision-making about the initiation of action and the employment of forces. The capacity of the European force to act separately in an extreme contingency would enable the United States to reserve decision whether to actually bring its European NATO contingent into action. Once the combined force had been activated, however, political control over its further employment would have to pass into the hands of the European political authority, in the interest of preserving the utility of the arrangement as a device for limiting conflict.

Two considerations might induce the United States to authorize the use of specifically earmarked forces and to surrender political control over their employment. First, the combined force of NATO-in-Europe might be sufficiently strong to deal with any but a total onslaught by the Soviet Union; this would reduce the need for committing the bulk of home-based American forces. Second, a limited United States involvement might be acceptable to the Soviet Union and keep the enlarged European force from triggering a pre-emptive Soviet response against the territorial United States; this might be the case as long as the exchange inflicted comparable damage on the Western side (including the committed American forces) and the Soviet side, and as long as the inactive bulk of American forces were sufficiently on the alert to deter the Soviets from escalating the conflict. Western defense would acquire a new form of flexibility, supplementing the flexibility found in capacity for counter-force strategy and conventional as well as tactical-nuclear defense. Alliance solidarity would be assured by the particularly intimate co-ordination between the European force and a segment of American forces. But the United States would be able to effect a measure of disengagement from Europe. Its residual presence there in the guise of nuclear and conventional forces assigned to NATO-in-Europe should suffice to perform their vital functions: as tokens of a continuing American commitment to Europe and as guarantors of the continuing commitment of Western Europe to NATO, as long as the two commitments are in the interest of the two parties and of global stability.

Co-ordinated in one way or another with United States

forces, a European nuclear force would not decrease the American capacity to act effectively against a Soviet attack on Europe; and it would increase the freedom of the United States to act nearer home. The least that can be said for the European deterrent is that it would increase by a small, but perhaps decisive, margin the reluctance of the Soviets to strike punitively in Europe while the United States was frustrating them elsewhere. International stability rests to a large extent on the impossibility of anticipating the results and consequences of a nuclear strike. The introduction of a separate European nuclear capability as a novel factor in the nuclear equation would promote such stability by complicating further the calculations of military-political challenge and response between the two original superpowers.

The eventual emergence of Communist China as yet another nuclear power may be accelerated by effective Chinese self-help or retarded by Soviet self-interest; but the event is independent of evolutions within the NATO alliance. The existence of a deterrent force in friendly hands might then be as welcome to the United States as the growth of the American navy ultimately was to the British when faced with the proliferation of naval power in potentially hostile hands. It might release the United States from the necessity of adhering to the nuclear equivalent of a two-power standard. The existence of a separate European deterrent might give rise to intimations that the American role in the defense of Europe was reduced or terminated; but even this would not significantly reduce the margin of additional restraint on the Soviet Union. The American strategic interest in Western Europe, however armed and organized, is too vital to guarantee inaction in a crisis. In return, the possession of an independent deterrent would serve to chasten the Euro-

peans. It would reduce to zero the possibility that the Western Europeans would not be defended despite their wish to
be defended at all costs. They would have the means of doing
so; and themselves to blame if they did not use them.

A separate European deterrent, without reducing the
capacity of the United States to act, would reduce the doubts
of Europeans about America's will to act by raising doubts
about their own; and it would reduce the quandary of the
United States regarding conventional forces by presenting
the Europeans with a nuclear dilemma of their own.

The Europeans have been accused of lacking the determination to increase their conventional forces, despite a
growing economic capacity to do so. But the United States
has hindered the one development which could make the
Europeans face up to the dilemma implicit in overreliance
on one's own nuclear capability, an overreliance which made
the United States rediscover the need for conventional forces
in the first place. There is a paradox here and a potential
harmony. The will to assume the cost for greater conventional armaments comes only when the still greater costs of
nuclear development have been undertaken, only to reveal
the need for conventional alternatives. By the time the European governments have come thus by the will, or political
capacity, to impose and share both cost burdens, the economic capacity of the Europeans to bear the costs of diversi-
fied defense will probably have been assured by the intervening rise in productivity and income. Only an autonomous
Western Europe will ever be ready to utilize fully her material
and demographic equality with the Soviet Union.

There are risks in any policy; and an innovation is doubly
unpalatable if it combines new risks with the diminution
of old privileges—those of control in this case. The United

States might be readier to accept both the risks and the diminution of control implicit in an independent nuclear European force if it became manifest that apparent alternatives entailed still greater risks without compensating advantages. The alternative instrument of United States policy has apparently become the project of a sea-borne multilateral NATO missile force with multinational crews, designed to associate the non-nuclear NATO powers with the nuclear ones, and especially with the United States. As planned, the not too big but still substantial multilateral force is to be jointly financed, manned, and managed; and it is to be jointly controlled, subject to a continuing American veto and continuing integration with United States strategic forces, thus ruling out independent employment. The modalities and the form of sharing control have remained uncertain; no less controversial have been the motives, incidental objectives, and likely consequences of the American initiative put forward as a means to enhance Atlantic solidarity and to give the non-American members a share in nuclear responsibilities.

The policy of separate national or European deterrents might fail, and the failure might undermine the morale necessary for any kind of European role in alliance strategy. Or the policy might succeed in too intense an opposition to the United States, and divide the alliance. By contrast, the policy of a multilateral nuclear NATO force might divide Western Europe, regardless of its being actually implemented as a meaningful departure from the existing pattern of responsibility for nuclear defense. The danger is especially great if the key European nation in the multilateral force should eventually be West Germany. This probability would become a certainty if France continued to bar her participation and Britain were debarred from taking a major part in the force by the already heavy cost of her stake in the parallel multinational, and so far only Anglo-American, nuclear deterrent force.

The multilateral force has been suggested as an alternative to the stationing of any medium-range ballistic missiles in West Europe and, specifically, on West German soil. Accordingly, the device would divert into multilateral channels German demands for an increased role in nuclear defense. But West Germany's preponderant material contribution to the multilateral force, and the decentralized nature of the sea-borne force, may turn out to be more compelling arguments for an increased share in control for the Bonn government than the location of tactical or strategic nuclear weapons on West German soil; and growing experience in handling vehicles of delivery may well stimulate interest in the possession or control of nuclear warheads as the logical next step in the rise of West Germany to equal status in the alliance.

Progress toward equality for West Germany is probably unavoidable and may be desirable; but the multilateral force might still make it premature and be unwise in form. In its timing, the American scheme has preceded a compelling expression of German desire for a nuclear role. This anticipation is fraught with graver risks than is that imputed to de Gaulle, when he appeared to foster German national pride to match French nationalism within a shared European emotion. The difference between the two anticipations in time points to the crucial question of form: whether military and political rehabilitations in the present go hand in hand with the crystallization of a firm, practically irreversible political commitment for the future.

As it stands, the project of a multilateral force has been linked with an Atlantic orientation that has been kept vague by the American sponsors of the force themselves. Should a major change occur, and the United States prove willing at some future date to bow out of the arrangement and surrender control over the force to the European members, the multilateral force would still not be a promising approach to Western European unity. European unification has flourished so far only in functional sectors such as the economic one, where NATO has served as no more than a protective shield and the United States has not been an integral partner and the directing spirit. Moreover, the multilateral force is defended with the contention that it is possible or necessary to progress from a nuclear force associating American and European components to a European political community and then to a European nuclear force. It is by inverting this order that one finds the most promising sequence of events. The outlook for unity may be affected by two kinds of conflict: a conflict to be avoided and a conflict that has already materialized. The desire to avoid the conflicts that can be expected to result from an uncontrolled development of national nuclear forces in Western Europe would probably work for political unity. A multilateral force run by the United States and organized around West Germany in the face of French opposition would give rise to real conflicts and suspicions that might indefinitely sidetrack the unification process before it got underway.

The calamity is made all the more likely by a related defect in the American design. The design lacks both a plausible core-power around which unity may be built and the potential for promoting unity by way of interaction between two smaller preliminary associations. West Germany would not be the ideal core-power under conditions that would permit recourse from revived suspicions to remedial measures and alignments. The other approach by way of two unification centers is no more promising. It failed spectacularly in Germany, since Prussia was not willing to concede lastingly, and Austria to be satisfied with, predominance in Germany south of the river Main. The approach might have some basis in historical, strategic, and economic realities if the preliminary unions in Europe were to evolve first around France and Great Britain, despite the danger of placing West Germany in the position of a balance wheel vis-à-vis France and Britain, a position which Bavaria occasionally sought to occupy between Prussia and Austria. But the approach would be disastrous if the two poles of unity were to be represented by West Germany, placed in a special relationship to the United States, and France, impelled to court the Iberian powers, to engage prematurely in a policy of equilibrium with the Eastern European powers, or to seek a resumption of the *entente cordiale* with a simultaneously alienated Britain.

The Soviets might be expected to respond with increased pressures to any new opportunities presented to them by this kind of strain in trans-Atlantic relations. But, independently of such opportunities, the pressures would also reflect traditional Soviet apprehensions. A West Germany moving toward a significant nuclear capability outside a restraining political framework would be doubly threatening to the Soviet Union. The direct threat at the exposed western boundary of the Soviet bloc might well be compounded by an indirect one on the eastern confines of Soviet Russia should German pressure eventually be added to that of the other irredentist great power with territorial claims on Russia, Communist China. In the 1920's, the German Army command co-operated with the Red Army in order to keep an elite in touch with evolving military technology in spite of treaty limitations, while keeping open political options for the future. The Soviets could not be blamed if they refused to gamble on the chance that the experience obtained in the multilateral force might again be turned ultimately against the power which made the initiation possible.

The untoward consequences of the multilateral-force or any other comparable design would be intensified if the design were to be implemented as a device for isolating France in Western Europe and defeating her bid for leadership. The probability that a deliberately divisive policy would succeed is less than the probability that it would compromise European unity regardless of whether it succeeded or failed. The success of the trans-Atlantic policy is doubtful as long as economic interests in the European Common Market and a sense of European solidarity against outsiders go on reinforcing one another. They work for a reintegrative response to a danger of disintegration originating in Western Europe; they will tend to work against forces that are suspect of being directed from outside Europe against disliked forms of European co-operation. The multilateral force may be designed to compete with the Common Market by offering an alternative framework for military integration to West Germany, Italy, and the lesser countries, and to facilitate, incidentally, the extension of the economic benefits of the Common Market across the Atlantic. An adverse balance of payments has led the United States to exact heavy financial contributions from the European participants in the multilateral force; impossibility to escape material burdens one way or the other is likely, however, to weight the balance of pressures perversely against the American and for an indigenous European concept of defense and unity.

Within the field of diffuse forces, pressures, and sentiments, the critical attitudes will be those of the lesser European states and of West Germany. Britain's orientation might become crucial only if she abandoned an independent nuclear role and adopted wholeheartedly the multilateral force as a vehicle for revamping the military side of her special relationship with the United States, at the price of generalizing such relationship up to a point. Even a Labor government might find it difficult to embrace such a policy wholeheartedly. Or the prospect of competing with West Germany over the position of principal European ally of the United States might incline Britain toward a European policy with France, a reaction which even a supine government might not be able to withstand under public pressure.

The lesser European countries might be attracted to a design such as that of the multilateral force if it were necessary and usable as an alternative to a Franco-German condominium that would dictate the terms of Western European unity. Where genuine, the fear of such a condominium has been unnecessary. Smaller powers lose in influence but gain in security and stability when the greater ones act in unison. Unity in Western Europe cannot be made lasting unless France and West Germany find a common ground for action. But to constitute a real threat, a Franco-German axis would have to display a very special unity, that of domineering purpose. Such unity is, however, at variance with France's need for the lesser states to assure her lasting equality with Germany and with Germany's need to respect the feelings of extra-continental countries that are vital for

her trade and defense and, as well, to respect the fears of
Eastern Europe in the hope of achieving national unity by
peaceful means. In any event, it would be a questionable
remedy for a Franco-German condominium to add a preponderant role in a nuclear force to West Germany's already
great conventional military role in NATO.

   The proponents of the multilateral force in the United
States seem to believe that, by its agency, they can perform
the feat of increasing the cohesion of a defensive alliance,
NATO, while promoting the pursuit of specific agreements
with the alliance's declared adversary, the Soviet Union. The
inheritors of Adenauer's authority in Bonn seem, in turn, to
believe that, by combining association with the United States
in the multilateral force, sponsorship of Britain's immediate
entry into the Common Market, and a *bonne et belle alliance*
with the declared opponent of both, France, they can maintain an even-handed friendship with all of the presently
divided powers of the West. Anxious, as if in expiation of
the disasters that a German regime wrought in Europe, to
have the approval of all, they risk ending with the respect
and support of none; and anxious to avoid most conceivable
risks, as if in reaction to the memory of the culpable regime
that had taken too many, they move in the direction of
one real danger. They may discover, too late for effecting
changes of policy within a Western framework, the impossibility of combining indefinitely palpable tokens of security
for rump-Germany with the partly intangible political preconditions of national unity and European reconstruction
within the compass of a single expedient, single-mindedly
devoted to the promotion of German objectives, such as
NATO was expected to be in the past. Where the United
States can hardly succeed in realizing two conflicting goals

by means of a single device of intra-alliance strategy, West Germany is still less likely to attain three not entirely or immediately complementary objectives by balancing between two contrasting unification strategies.

The West Germans may go on trying to associate the United States with their national predicament in the face of an unyielding East, just as Britons have tried with respect to their imperial predicament in the face of an ascendant part of the European West. But the real predicament is one which the United States has come to share with Western Europe. The unity of Western Europe can no longer be brought about by the United States; it must probably be accomplished, to some extent, in opposition to the United States in the sense of being an act of self-differentiation from America. But if the United States on its part continues to oppose separate nuclear forces for Europeans, the growing material burden of independent effort will make it increasingly imperative to stress the particular national function of the capability in order to mobilize support in national pride and resentment. The nationalist potential of such an attempt is manifest; so is the alternative to it, political apathy as a result of defeat and renunciation.

A French nuclear force alone, or collaboration in the production and control of nuclear warheads and the means of delivery between two or more greater Western European states, might be the military basis of European political unity. The initially non-participating states would find it easier to rally around the spearhead power or powers, from the viewpoint of their security as well as prestige, if the United States assisted, directly or indirectly, the establishment of such a force. For the United States to attach stipulations regarding political unity would be neither desirable nor

necessary; the mere fact of outside assistance would render
the European nuclear power or powers less able to resist
strictly European pressures for equitable nuclear sharing
and joint political control. All spearhead powers can be
expected to accept, sooner or later, both extra-European
assistance and the European consequences of such assistance.
None would willingly incur the material disadvantage of
perpetuating unnecessary economic burdens for its nation
and the moral disadvantage of driving potential partners in
unity into countervailing trans-Atlantic or other policies
against their will.

The United States can have enough confidence in itself
and its indispensable role in the West to let go of waning
direct controls over Western Europe. Unless they are pro-
voked into untoward reprisals, the most independence-
minded Europeans can be relied upon to know that small
and imperfect weapons systems are not militarily and politically sufficient even if they are not militarily and politically
useless. A United States true to its democratic commitment
can have only one overriding foreign-policy purpose with
regard to Western Europe: to retain her as an effective ally
until the revolutionary drive of the Communist powers has
subsided or the evolutionary possibilities of an Atlantic Community have matured. For both purposes, a self-confident
Western Europe is preferable to a demoralized and divided
one. It ought to be preferred by the United States even if it
resembles the so-called Gaullist Europe more than the Monnet Europe that faltered whenever supranational integration
was to spill over from economics into the political and military domains. A measure of defection of a confederate Europe from the rudimentary Atlantic union was inevitable
once the United States did not promote closer Atlantic unity

in the period of its unquestioned moral and material sway. Atlantic unity is unlikely to progress significantly as long as the alternation in the economic fortunes of the two branches of the West continues to put one or the other at a relative disadvantage at critical junctures. The next great opportunity for Atlantic unity may come only when the dilemmas implicit in the juxtaposition of self-sufficient and separate, but mutually not truly independent, American and European nuclear capabilities in the face of other nuclear powers will recommend unity as an alternative to separate or even reciprocal destructions.

Western Europe and Global Stability

If it is difficult to guarantee the military efficacy of a particular defense or armaments policy, it is virtually impossible to predict with certainty the political effects and potentialities of such policies. The uncertainty can be reduced only by placing the immediate military-political problem in the widest possible context. The context of our problem is the expectations regarding the future role and orientation of a united Western Europe in the world at large, to be inferred in part from the changing character and style of international relations.

Western Europe is too important a part of the world system to escape the influence of predominating structural trends. The course and outcome of World War II have manifestly favored big entities for welfare and defense; but, more recently, there has been a tendency toward a loosening of the conglomerates of rigid bipolarity. The more recent trend has completed the cycle begun in the colonial domains, which had been disrupted in large part as a result of the conflict underlying bipolarity; and it has revived political patterns and diplomatic behavior which are associated with the multiple state system and which have only been modified by revolutions in weaponry and in the organization and management of resources.

The emerging state of things may be more delicate, politically and militarily, than was that of the delicate balance of terror poised upon the insufficiently protected but centrally controlled nuclear forces of the two superpowers. But it is also more hopeful, insofar as it adjoins to the continued pressure of effective power new opportunities for the reordering of quasi-colonial relationships at the center of the international system. As the blocs loosen up, there is still need for skills in organizing resources within seemingly permanent agglomerates among unequally powerful and independent parties. But these skills become again no more precious than is virtuosity in diplomatic maneuver with respect to a growing number of relatively independent, both friendly and adversary, powers. Faculties that went, in the West, into epochal ventures such as the Marshall Plan, NATO as an integrated alliance, and the European economic communities will not go into discard; but they would be a handicap if overrelied upon as the wave of the future, because of distaste for the ever-problematic nature of international politics as an art and, frequently, improvised art.

The United States has had a key role in these evolutions and has a stake in adapting itself to them. The postwar organizational designs were fostered by the conjunction of America's particular genius and global bipolarity; the reemergence of the old-new patterns of diplomatic flexibility has been accelerated by American material assistance, in part tied into the programs. The United States has now to draw the consequences from its success. It must henceforth act with the awareness that neither the military-technological nor the institutional and economic revolutions have been sufficiently thoroughgoing in their effect on international relations; and that, therefore, alliances of nations cannot be handled indefinitely as if they were business corporations, allocating functions by the principle of efficiency and rationality only. The unity of Western Europe and the defense of the West are not technical problems which can be approached by way of belated nuclear adaptations of the design for a European Defense Community. The time has passed when Europeans can be usefully initiated into the mysteries of nuclear weaponry as part of a carefully graduated education toward conditional emancipation and unity at a later stage.

Being political problems, moreover, unity and defense of sovereign states cannot be treated as if they were issues of domestic policy, even before there is an Atlantic community. Such policy rests habitually on two major assumptions. One assumption is that of continued and sufficient control by the dominant authority; another is that of continuing or recurrent opportunities for gradual or decisive action, while alternative options are kept open, disparate interests are reconciled, and most or all immediate risks are carefully avoided. Instead, political evolutions in Western Europe have been rapidly becoming critical foreign-policy problems. Such problems rule out continuous control and offer unique opportunities for decisive action with roughly calculable but never avoidable immediate and long-range risks.

In these conditions, the role of integration is likely to change. Military integration may be more important in the sphere of production than in that of deployment of the components of a coherent defense capability. It may not be considerable even in the reduced scope between allies, such as the Atlantic ones, that do not contemplate closer political association in the foreseeable future. But joint research and production between the European allies, say Franco-German co-operation in the field of ballistics or Anglo-French co-operation in that of nuclear warheads and nuclear-powered submarines, might constitute the military counterpart to economic integration and encourage the co-ordination of political policies. As part of political integration, individual determination of formal foreign policies, concerned with "interdependence" or "independence" in nuclear defense, and of negative foreign policies, concerned with prevention of one another's real or suspected objectives in Europe, would give way to a new pattern. The pattern would be that of joint determination of specific, positive, and in a new way world-wide policies.

Just as the internal and external conditions of Western European unity are a compound of old and new factors, so are the perspectives which would present themselves to a united Western Europe in the world at large. None of these perspectives is necessarily in conflict with immediate and long-range American interests. The perspectives extend in the West toward the United States and, if she chooses the Atlantic over the Channel, Great Britain; in the East toward the Soviet Union and, with it, the Central-Eastern European states as well as Communist China; and in the South toward North Africa and, beyond her, Africa as a whole.

These are all areas and powers which played a crucial part in the traditional balance-of-power politics of disunited Europe, as more or less active and independent regulators of the balance from the outside or more or less controlled and passive weights. Military manpower from Africa was the most passive of weights; it compensated France, in particular, for backsliding in national capabilities. The active, regulatory function was systematically exercised only by Britain, the one power that was as dependent on the state of the continent for its military security as it was culturally independent as a society. In its relation to Europe in the remoter past, the United States resembled the other land mass, Russia in the East, more than it resembled the British island power. Both giant countries were more independent from Europe militarily than culturally, and both affected European politics as decisive but unpredictable weights. They converged on Europe directly as well as indirectly by gaining strength as well as enemies through their ostensibly divergent continental expansions. The chief sufferer from the convergence, consummated in World War II, was, along with the European balance-of-power system, the state that had interpreted the requirements of the balance to the advantage of both of the two wing powers in at least some periods of their weakness and growth. The delicate regulatory function of Great Britain was permanently broken up. By contrast, the European system of states may have been disrupted only temporarily, while the potential of Western Europe as a power in the global system was probably damaged least fatally.

A global system can be regulated only from within itself; it must be self-regulating or not be regulated at all. As a power in the global system, Western Europe can play an enlarged role if, along with progress in unification and in the generation of economic values and political energies, she can evolve updated policies toward her neighbors. This

means different things in the westward, eastward, and southward direction; but it calls in each case for emotional emancipation from the past as well as for intellectual adaptation
of past patterns.

We need only restate, in general terms, the key problem
in the relations between Western Europe and the United
States. The relationship will continue to be a vital one as
both parties evolve a new balance in their emphasis on
organization and diplomacy, nationalism and supranationality. It is America's turn now to give up the attitude
of protector, if not colonizer, vis-à-vis Western Europe just
as the European states had successively to give up a similar
attitude toward the North American continent. The attend-
ant strains will shrink into insignificance as either still larger
transformations take place in relations among the world
powers or as the United States and Western Europe converge
toward closer unity on new terms, if the present global conflict continues and culminates essentially unchanged. The
new terms of such association would merely formalize the
influence which the European political tradition exerted on
American foreign policy even during the period of Europe's
material eclipse and America's unchallenged ascendancy in
the West.

More delicate in form and going deeper in substance are
the adjustments that might first regularize and then reshape
relations between Western Europe and Soviet Russia. Russia
and the great European states to the west of her share a long
history of both peaceful and warlike coexistence. But they
have so far mainly feared each other as a threat or em-
barrassed one another as allies against culturally closer but
politico-militarily more immediately dangerous powers. Russia felt threatened by all the surviving major powers of

Europe in succession: by France, briefly and spectacularly; by England, longer if less conspicuously; and by Germany, most recently and most cruelly. Russia loomed as a threat to Western Europe ever since the partition of Poland; the threat has reached its climax with the subjection of Central-Eastern Europe and the partition of Germany. As an embarrassing ally, Russia served Britain against France, a power culturally closer to Britain and more authentically European than Russia; and both France and Britain were in a similarly denatured alliance with Russia against a Prussia-centered Germany that was in many respects closer to both the Western powers and their Eastern ally than they were to one another. Russia's experience in particular alliances was thus not always entirely satisfactory even when it was materially profitable. By contrast, her occasional participation in the European concert tended to be more flattering than rewarding—a state of things which interplayed as both cause and effect with Russia's remaining foreign-policy options: pursuit of direct control in areas adjoining her western frontier and expansion eastward, away from Europe and toward Asian and global horizons.

The ideological cleavage that was advanced into the middle of the European continent by the latest German war has seemed to aggravate the historical alienation beyond repair. But as the division endures without precipitating either conquest or conflagration, it may help narrow gradually the gap between Europe's West and East—by making reciprocal inferiority and superiority feelings less acute and the technological aspects of culture less divergent. The sum of truly galling differences between Western Europe and Russia may already have decreased from what it had been while Europe constituted a single system of states; and the

remaining differences may be less significant in the longer
run than are the cultural affinities of Western and Eastern
Europe relative to the Asian East and their geopolitical
unity relative to the extensions of the two halves of Europe
westward and eastward. With the aid of outside pressures,
the idea and process of continental unity might yet spread
from Western Europe eastward and do so in an intensified
form, just as did other strands in the continent's political
culture, including nationalism and socialism.

A meaningful rapprochement between Western and Eastern Europe is likely to be the product of evolutions in the
Sino-Soviet bloc and in the world at large, rather than the
product of a diplomatic coup in Europe alone. Trends in
this direction have been only tentative and can still be reversed, among other things, by the Western Europeans and
the Americans engaging in premature competition over who
would be the first to enter into a privileged relationship with
the Soviet Union. Such a competition is less likely to take
place, the more manifest it is that neither side is disposed to
seek or able to achieve the stance feared by the other side—
that of a neutralist third force for Western Europe and that
of the second party to a world-encompassing deal for the
United States.

The third-force implications of Western European unity
have been disquieting to the United States even before the
event, somewhat as the honest-broker attitude of Bismarck
disturbed the Russian patron of Prussia-Germany soon after
unification. By dampening the extreme pretensions of the
Prussian military (supported by the King) and rejecting the
pretensions of Russian diplomacy (backed by the Tsar),
Bismarck tried to show that the new Germany would be
neither an expansionist power in the South and West nor a

dependent of the older Empire in the East; in short, that she was disposed to be both secure and stable, and both stable and potentially stabilizing. The situation changed only when the *Weltpolitik* of the successors of Bismarck magnified the consequences of Bismarck's own one departure from moderation and played into the hands of the French policy of revenge.

There are parallels in the statecraft of the contemporary proponent of Western European unity and independence. Soviet propaganda notwithstanding, de Gaulle's rejection of American patronage could not but be pleasing to the Soviets, provided that France can succeed in her attempt to simultaneously lean on, back, and moderate West Germany politically. And de Gaulle's firm, if tactically nuanced, opposition to Soviet sway in Central-Eastern Europe in its present form could not but reassure the United States and all those who wish for a Europe that would again be both one and reasonably free. There is a great difference between such a policy and either passive non-alignment between the two superpowers or an overactive neutralist policy of playing off one superpower against the other. In the mid-1940's de Gaulle turned to Stalin, since Roosevelt had turned him down as a respected ally and Churchill as an intimate ally. The Soviets treated France no more respectfully than did her Western allies just because she had the past and perhaps future potential of a strong land power, useful as ally against a revanchist Germany. In the foreseeable future it is unlikely that either de Gaulle or any other responsible European statesman would, of his own accord, seek to do more in the nuclear context than resume Western Europe's dialogue with the Soviets that would match America's.

But, if American precautions against a Western Europe

that would be capable of diplomatic initiatives of her own are largely unnecessary, have European suspicions of the United States been warranted? As the challenger's drive for supremacy falters, the leader of the defensive coalition is faced with an awkward choice. He can seek an understanding with the challenger, perhaps at the expense of lesser allies and certainly at the risk of alienating them prematurely, or he can resign himself to forfeiting some of the fruits of success, as ties in the defensive alliance grow lax and lesser allies qualify for a separate accommodation with the antagonist. The desire to escape the unpalatable choice releases energies that may be or may appear to be hegemonic. Britain's separate-peace propensities damaged her reputation as coalition-leader even more than her intermittent dictatorship over her rimland allies, which stopped short of the hegemony exerted by another naval power, Athens. The exigencies of leadership in conditions of endemic crisis become harder to accept as the leadership comes to be challenged. The resulting strain has occasionally threatened the moral resolve of the United States to go on managing the alliance as an association of free partners. The danger may not be great; but it is greater than has been the danger so far for the United States of a rapprochement between France or West Germany and the Soviet Union or the danger of an American-Soviet understanding for the Western Europeans.

The relationship of forces between the two rival superpowers will be as difficult or impossible to stabilize by concerted limitation and control of the arms race as it would be by formal delimitation of territorial spheres of political control. Lasting agreements on the terms of something like condominium become desirable between major competitors when they are apparently necessary; but by that time they are no longer possible. As long as two major powers control the situation, agreement between them is defeated by each party regarding every possible gain of the adversary as a certain loss for himself, and by each postponing the real or suspected liabilities of agreement so long as he can hope to win all. Agreement becomes more attractive when other powers come into the picture and seek to rival the major contestants; but it is likely to be frustrated even then. A third power that is strong enough to exert pressures is also attractive enough for at least one of the original contenders as an alternative partner in an arrangement, and it is likely to have enough capacity to nullify the bearing of any agreement between the two original contestants as a basis of a new world order. It is unlikely that there would be no contemporary validity in propositions which find support in political logic and in historical events as remote from one another as the peace treaty between the Athenian and the Persian empires in the middle of the fifth century B.C. and the Anglo-French negotiations over partitioning the Spanish succession at the end of the seventeenth century.

As long as the Soviets hold onto their leadership in the Communist bloc, they are unlikely to make any substantial concessions to the American viewpoint. The desire to avert a politically safeguarded diffusion of nuclear weaponry to Western Europe would hardly overcome Soviet distaste for an internationally supervised arms-control agreement. Rather than incite the Soviets to pass on nuclear weapons and information to Communist China, such diffusion might merely intensify the already existing tensions between the Communist allies on this issue. Should the Sino-Soviet alliance finally break up, the Soviets might be ready for major adjustments in policy. The United States is the logical part-

ner for the Soviet Union as a major nuclear power seeking
a *détente;* but Western Europe would be the more interesting
partner for a politically weakened and Europeanized Soviet
Union anxious to avoid a diplomatic encirclement.

The loss of a major ally, even of one that has become
something of a liability, hurts not only the morale but also
the security of the deserted power. The loss is greater if
the ally guards vulnerable approaches to national territory,
helps project influence into otherwise less accessible regions,
and might become a claimant against the deserted power or
might fall under the influence or control of its adversaries
once it stops being an ally. The relationship of the Soviet
Union with China is comparable in at least some of these
respects with earlier relationships and frictions between
Bourbon France and Spain in the Family Compact and
between Imperial Germany and the Austro-Hungarian Empire in the Dual Alliance. To escape inferiority vis-à-vis the
United States, a Soviet Union that has just been severed from
Communist China would have an interest in depriving the
United States of its political monopoly in Western Europe;
and to escape the danger of being wedged between two irredentist powers, West Germany and China, the Soviet Union would have an interest in satisfying basic German demands within a new European order before the natural
identity of interests between the two dissatisfied neighbors
of the Soviet empire would assert itself over ideological and
other differences. The task of the Soviets would be an easier
one if the Europeans had meanwhile come to resent American insistence on retaining a however disguised nuclear
monopoly.

The utility or futility of a dynamic European policy can
be meaningfully argued only in terms of propositions about

basic policy prospects and principles. One such proposition would have it that, in a situation that is not rigidly polarized between two powers, ambivalent, competitive-co-operative relations among powers become possible and even normal. This would mean in practice that a united Western Europe could have both a measure of military-political autonomy in relation to the United States and continue to be guaranteed by the United States against unprovoked Soviet aggression. It would mean that this kind of guarantee would be acceptable to the United States so that Western Europe might be able both to go on counterbalancing the Soviet Union in association with the United States and to seize upon opportunities for relations or arrangements with the Soviet Union which, while consonant with principal American objectives, would not necessarily include the United States as a party to them. And it would mean, finally, that under such arrangements France and perhaps Great Britain would seek to strengthen themselves by association with West Germany with regard to the Soviet Union while achieving an understanding with the Soviet Union and the lesser Central-Eastern European states directed toward restraining West Germany from the pursuit of lost unity, and an eventually united Germany from the pursuit of lost territory and influence, by disruptive means or with destabilizing results.

The other, related proposition bears on the relationship of pressure and receptivity to response. If a major power cannot be brought to make major concessions by pressure alone, it becomes necessary to provide at the same time also a receptacle for concessions, in the form of institutional structures or alignments that make the concessions both acceptable in terms of prestige, by saving face, and of policy, by restricting the bearing of the concession and opening the prospects of compensating new departures and opportunities. The proposition gives rise to two questions in contemporary practice: Firstly, whether the United States could accept the reorganization of Western pressure on the Soviet Union in such a way as to allow for Western European military-political autonomy. And secondly, whether the supplementary Western deterrent can be so organized as to constitute simultaneously the second component of the total policy. Such a component would be a European political structure that would be superior to the Atlantic Alliance and to the United States itself as a politically attractive and structurally flexible recipient for Soviet concessions. The critical concessions could not but lie in the domain of Soviet controls in a Central-Eastern Europe that would have ceased to be useful as a springboard against a no longer weak Western Europe or necessary as a rampart against a no longer sheerly antagonistic military and political constellation in Western Europe.

Autonomous developments in Western Europe would diversify the range of possible Western responses to developments within the Sino-Soviet bloc in the interest of long-range political stability. It is impossible to see far ahead with clarity; but it is safe to assume that contemporary preoccupations relating to the triangular relationship between the United States, a united Western Europe, and the Soviet Union are not of a permanent nature. They would be substantially modified in a world system that would consist of a plurality of major powers susceptible of acting in formal or tacit concert and approximating the conditions of shared deterrence from war, absorption in internal growth, and utilized outlets abroad that made such a concert possible in the past.

A working concert requires that there be more than two members and that the principal powers be both linked and insulated from each other by other strong powers, as Britain and Russia were in the nineteenth century. Contemporary trends toward a tacit concert can be durably strengthened only by the rise of Western Europe as an independent party, by a symmetric loosening of ties within the Sino-Soviet bloc, and, if less importantly, by the emergence of other first-class actors in international politics. Sino-Soviet differences are most likely to deepen if the two Communist powers are unable to gain significant new successes abroad and the inability aggravates their divergencies regarding the objectives that can be pursued at the risk of war in a nuclear environment. The loosening of ties within both blocs is to an unequal extent a function of the East-West conflict. But that same relaxing of ties is probably also a precondition of the conflict not culminating in a climactic confrontation within the time-span that is the concern of contemporary statecraft. It is unlikely that a merely military stability can stand indefinitely the strain of a conflict that, in nuclear terms, would remain one between two powers.

Whether the blocs break up or not, the essential character of the ultimate confrontation might still be the same, however. In both eventualities, the East-West conflict of ideology and power threatens to be aggravated by, or even transmuted into, a conflict that previous generations spoke of as one between Europe and Asia. Even had there been no European colonialism, the awakening of the non-European world was bound to introduce the racial dimension into conflicts of interests among states, just as nationality aggravated conflicts following the French Revolution. The two blocs cannot probably be retightened now without the Sino-Soviet bloc being Sinified in spirit and purpose at least as much as the Western Alliance is likely to be progressively Europeanized in the determination of policy. If the other major possibility occurs, and the Sino-Soviet bloc disintegrates, an intermediary *détente* and concert may be the first result. But, should it occur, the reversion of Soviet Russia to the European fold would make it easier for a meanwhile strengthened China to secure the political leadership of Communist Asia. From such a base, China could hope to exploit resentments in those Afro-Asian countries that would have decayed politically and failed to develop economically in the meantime.

Trends toward a global conflict along racial lines can best be mitigated by preserving interests and affinities that survived colonial connections or that have been established in the contemporary phase of the East-West conflict. Here would belong the countervailing attraction which the United States and the formerly imperial European powers might go on exercising in the new countries of Asia and Africa, in unison or in truly peaceful competition, and the pull which a reconstituted Western Europe might exert especially in her immediate vicinity to the south. The natural and crucial arena of such attraction for Western Europe lies in Africa and, most of all, in North Africa.

North Africa will be politically important for Western Europe and Western Europe will be economically important for North Africa in any global conditions that can be envisaged at present. In any such conditions, too, the recasting of the relations between the North African countries, individually and collectively, Western Europe in general, and France in particular may prove to be more difficult even than the recasting of relations between Western and Eastern Europe. The basic conditions of such a recasting have been created, however. They call forth one more analogy. Prussia had to get rid of the deadweight of Austria and of the German Confederation before Prussia could be fitted into Germany and before Germany could enter into a quasi-constitutional international alliance with Austria-Hungary. Similarly, the Fifth Republic had first to liquidate France's liability in the south, in the form of French Algeria and the still-born French Union, before France could turn her full attention to Western Europe and before Western Europe could be ready for a revised relation with the countries of the North African Maghreb. In both instances the historically and strategically related states in the south had to be kept from decay and disintegration, and out of the magnetic field of an Eastern alliance. In the pursuit of these tasks, neither Bismarck nor de Gaulle did or probably could shrink from alternately using and sacrificing the radical adherents of a larger, assimilationist unity: the German nationalists of Austria and the Europeans of French Algeria.

The Meeting of the Two Occidents

Relations between Western Europe and the part of North Africa called the Maghreb—meaning the Occident—have a very long past. At issue now is their future. The liquidation of the French empire in North Africa has opened the way for a new assessment of the colonial experience on both sides, while the relationship between former colonizer and colonized undergoes a radical change. Interpretations that flourished in the colonial period have become obsolete. The change in conditions has been more important for re-examinations on the formerly dominant side; the disproval

of interpretations by events matters more for the formerly
colonized party.

In the metropole, postcolonial demands for the reparation
of real or imagined past spoliations have been backed by
the moral kin of early opponents of imperialism. In the face
of these exactions, the temperamental kin of the early im-
perialists have tended to downgrade, statistics in hand, the
past economic utility of colonies for the dominant nation as a
whole. But the inclination to take a hard line with former
dependencies has been counteracted by another shift in
attitudes. Following formal emancipation, the former metropole has been trying to retain links with former dependents
mainly as a means to continued great-power status; this has
tended to recall the similarity of the original motives for
acquiring colonies in the late nineteenth century, before the
ever bigger metropolitan capitalists set out to dominate the
weak and win over the strong imperial proconsuls. The fact
that the connection was repoliticized after independence has
helped to sweep away the economic emphases of the golden
age of colonial capitalism.

The North Africans have found it harder to shed the economic interpretations of their past and present plight. A
politically significant refutation of the long attractive de-
terministic doctrine has occurred only as the new economic
vitality in both France and other Western European countries gave support to the feeling that, if necessary, Western
Europe could live and prosper without North Africa no less
than without other former dependencies in Africa and elsewhere; that whatever may have been true of earlier capitalism, the modern Western European economies could cope
with so-called contradictions without having nearly as great
an economic need of North Africa as North Africa had of

Western Europe. If Western Europe as a whole joins France in accepting largely dispensable products and diverts resources from her own underdeveloped areas to the former dependencies in North Africa and Africa as a whole, she will not go on doing it primarily in order to safeguard raw-material supplies, rich potential markets, and cheap labor power. The main object is rather to protect the West European underbelly from an enveloping political and military operation.

Western Europe has been moving into a position of strength with regard to the regions south of her, long before she could attain a comparable position westward and eastward. This fact is likely to have beneficial effects on relations between Western Europe and North Africa, enabling the Western Europeans to assume a liberal posture. And it will discourage the North Africans from indulging in retribution for the colonial past. Stretching the politically meaningful historical memory of men, it must suffice for the North Africans to see in the reconquest of independence in Algeria the crowning counterpart to the reconquest of Andalusia by the Spaniards from the Moslems five centuries ago. On such a basis of independence and, perhaps, unity for both sides, it ought to be possible to resume the interplay of the two fragments of the state system in the Western Mediterranean, interrupted by the period of French sway in the Maghreb.

While Western Europeans approached the business of unity as if they had reached the postnationalist stage, the North Africans have toyed with the idea of unity in a nationalist or even prenationalist climate of sentiment. Regional unity has attracted the leaders of Morocco, Tunisia, and Algeria as the only lastingly effective substitute for the colonial power, which opposed such unity while at the same time co-ordinating development in the region. In reality, however, North Africans have been reluctant to rush into commitments. This reluctance is in keeping with their traditional preference for flexible balancing of the greatest possible number of options, allies, and adversaries. The ideal environment for such politics has been a North Africa operating as a particular system of states in a larger state system, rather than as a regional unity expressing the geographic and cultural distinctiveness of the area.*

Like other geopolitically bounded fragments of the system of sovereign states, the Maghreb is defined by conflicts as much as by the solidarities which may mute the conflicts and by the alignments which may result from them. The principal conflicts defining the Maghreb have been of three closely related kinds. One class of conflict has been over space and resources, symbolized by the frontier; another class of con-

---

* The Western portion of North Africa, the so-called Maghreb, is a separate and self-contained geographic entity. The Maghrebian occidental island is set in two kinds of seas: the real seas of the Atlantic from the west and the Mediterranean from the north, and the seas of sand in the south and east. The eastern, Syrtic desert allocates the western part of the Libyan land archipelago to the Maghreb and thrusts Cyrenaica, the eastern province of Libya, toward Egypt. The Sahara in the south links the Maghreb arduously with Black Africa for both trade and, in the past, occasional invasion; but it constitutes no less a geographic and racial boundary, with the color line running so as to attribute to the "Arab" Maghreb the northern parts of Mauritania and of the Libyan Fezzan.

The key boundaries of the Maghreb thus run through contested Mauritania and internally strained Libya. Geographically, only the northwestern section of Libya is part of the Maghreb proper. As a state, Libya has been only marginally and uncertainly part of the Maghreb political system, and may become ever less so following Algerian independence. At the other extremity of the geographic Maghreb, Mauritania is linked to the North African political system mainly by Morocco's claims on Mauritania—one of the conflicts which define and structure the regional system.

flicts has been over effective control of space and resources, currently symbolized by decolonization. The first class of conflicts identifies the Maghreb as a system of separate and sovereign territorial states; the second, as a merely emergent system of states. The third class of conflicts, over regional leadership, identifies the Maghreb as a fragment of the state system with some form of unity as a vocation. Without depriving France of a special position, the decolonization struggle has brought outside powers into the politics of the region. At one time or another, the United States, the United Arab Republic, and the Sino-Soviet allies were the key regionally present powers. They played a more significant role than the African countries to the south, despite pan-African diplomatic fraternizing and economic daydreaming. But, as decolonization changes from a politico-military into an economic-development process, the power which comes to loom largest next to France is the European Economic Community as a whole.

It is natural for an Islamic North Africa organized for independent action to be linked with Christian Western Europe in a system of both conflict and collaboration. Neither the raids from North Africa southward nor the more lastingly significant surge from the Middle East westward would seem to match trans-Mediterranean relations in contemporary significance. In the past, the major patterns of relations were reciprocal conquest, organization, and rollback, as one or the other side fell victim to military imbalance, political splintering, and demoralization. But despite religious inhibitions, Moslem North Africa and Western Europe were also linked occasionally by short-lived complicities and alignments as by-products of struggles over succession, trade, and hegemony on both sides of the Mediterranean. A relatively recent example is the collusion of Tunis with France, which preceded the end of Ottoman dominance and the beginning of French sway in Algeria. This incident showed that, in a tripartite North African system, the weaker country would not hesitate to seek support outside the region, and most readily in Western Europe, especially if it could not have an effective alliance with the other North African wing power against expansionist subversive policies of the Algerian center.

With the restoration of independence, the Maghreb has been falling back into the patterns of a competitive regional system of three states (or, counting in Libya and Mauritania, four or five states). This development has imparted a certain plausibility to the aspiration to unity; but it has also helped to frustrate the implementation of a series of initiatives toward unity, both governmental and non-governmental, often inspired by the desire to consolidate the ephemeral advantage of one party or to share in the assets of another. Uncertainty about more basic goals has only aggravated the failures to live up to affirmations of solidarity. These have been some of the questions preoccupying the North Africans as they looked beyond independence: Should unity be merely economic or broadly political? Is unification to amount to a mere co-ordination of policies, to a loose confederation, or is it to be embodied in supranational institutions? Will the Maghreb be Arab, African or Mediterranean, great and united, or just united?

All the three principal countries have suffered from inadequate authority. While authority in Morocco has again come to be contested, it has been still unsettled in Algeria and already decaying in Tunisia. In the face of pervasive particularism, the main problem of Algeria has been to consolidate nationhood; that of Morocco to save the state and the political order from a dangerous tendency to polarization of political leaders and their mass support; and that of Tunisia to overcome political apathy and revitalize leadership. While the main problems of the two bigger countries have been political, Tunisia's problem of sheer survival has been at least as much an economic one. None of the North African governments has seemed able to assure more than the minimum economic viability of its country. One set of obstacles has been identified with continuing structural disequilibria between population and resources and between the traditional and the modern industrial and agricultural sectors; another continuing difficulty has been how to strike a workable balance between socialist policies, favored mainly in the agricultural sector, and capitalist policies, encouraged from conviction or tolerated out of necessity mainly in the industrial sector.

Whereas the economic predicaments of the three countries have been similar, their resources have been unequal. This has placed in doubt the possibility of evolving a satisfactory regional equilibrium in the future. Algeria's size, number of trained elites, and supply of industrial and mineral resources have made of the country the most widely favored candidate for an economically superior position, despite some reservations that have been reinforced by the depletions and maladjustments following independence. The economic advantage might be converted into political hegemony in the region, notably if the policy of subversion in the name of pan-Arabism were to predominate over the policy of sharing and co-ordinating material and energetic resources of the Sahara in particular. Even while asserting equanimity with regard to a possible Algerian threat, the governments of the two wing countries have actually been engaged in a series of strategies designed to strengthen their relative positions. The quest for diplomatic and material reinforcements by way of connections with African, Western, and Communist powers and by way of territorial claims within the Maghrebian compass has, however, militated against harmony within the region as well as against the political confinement of the region. Distracting outside connections have not been offset by concrete prospects for economic expansion by means of regional co-operation and unity.

The agitation of designs for functional economic co-operation in a North African common market has been at variance with the realities of non-complementary economies and non-co-operative economic policies. The absence of a considered unification strategy has been only highlighted by sporadic and ineffectual thrusts of the Moroccan government in the direction of creating economic and political *faits accomplis* that might bring the need for major new agreements into the field of practical politics; by tactical shifts of especially the Algerian and the Tunisian leaderships in their attitude to unity before and after Algerian independence; and by the tendency of oppositional groups, notably but not only in Morocco, to see in unity both a utopian remedy to chiefly economic ills and a highly practical device for recovering a share in political power.

On the whole, cultural and economic factors making for unity and political inhibitions to unity have been uneasily balancing one another. Other key factors have remained indeterminate in their effect on unification. Here belong the cleavage between Arab and Berber which continues to run through North Africa; the regional links and rivalries between national trade unions, student organizations, and other professional and functional groups; and last but not least, the resources of the Sahara. The role envisaged for the Sahara recalls the role that was contemplated for the Saar in the Western European, or Franco-German, unification process. The dream of formal co-sovereignty or condominium for the states adjoining the Sahara was the first to vanish; it may yet be followed by initial hopes for practical ways of sharing Saharan resources on a Meghrebian rather than so-called capitalist basis, as a neighborly right rather than a revocable payoff for diplomatic and other favors, now that the Algerians have thwarted attempts to apply the separatist Katanga formula against them. Frontier conflicts, fed by disappointments in regard to the sharing of oil and gas, might only be sharpened if water came to be drawn in large quantities from underneath the hitherto sterile desert.

Conflicts of this kind might either finally compel unity or intensify all the factors against it beyond the possibility of reintegrative response. Indeterminate factors, such as potentially shared resources and activities, can work for cohesion only as the more fundamental conditions of unity impart a momentum to the unification process. Until then they are part of the status quo and share its tendency to inertia or deterioration.

If, underneath much superficial agitation, the Maghreb remains much as it is, it will not really fall short of the sham unions which have been making fitful appearance in Africa. And one more fragmented area will merely reproduce the failure of the series of projects of unity rehearsed in the period between the world wars in Central-Eastern Europe. There, too, organic union was blocked by differences in more or less stable regimes as well as by antagonisms among key personalities and peoples, fed by suspicions of local imperialisms. The Central-Eastern European states, too, were open, or deliberately opened themselves, to conflicting pressures and apparently profitable alignments with outside powers in all directions. Lacking sufficient and sufficiently complementary economic resources, they depended for both political and economic support on different outside powers.

There is, however, a major difference. The Central-Eastern European states leaned politically on two groupings of powers neither of which was favorable to unity. The Western powers, France and Britain, pressed for regional unity for reasons of their own, but were unable to provide economic markets for the lesser countries individually or collectively; the Central-European powers, Italy and Germany, were apparently more capable of absorbing the export surplus of the lesser states, but were unwilling to support regional unity on any meaningful terms. The Western powers, and notably France, lacked the elements of constraint as well as inducement for unity; the Central powers, and notably Nazi Germany, would not induce unity since they wished to constrain separately. The North Africans have already experimented with leaning on remote and economically deficient powers. They can do better in the future than did the Central and Eastern Europeans, if they can count on proper politico-economic support and even a special kind of constraint from the Western powers, who presumably would be less divided and more resolute than they were in the period between the wars.

North Africa is not the only area where apprehensions regarding the European Common Market have already replaced opposition to military alliances as the rallying cry of anti-colonialism. The apprehensions have been nourished by somewhat contradictory suspicions. One suspicion is that the European Common Market might dominate North African economies by dictating terms of both trade and aid and keeping the Maghreb in the position of a raw-material producing dependent; in short, a united Western Europe is feared as potentially neo-colonialist. Another suspicion is that Western Europe might cut off the North Africans by no longer importing their foodstuffs and labor force, amply available in the European South; in short, she might turn out to be neo-isolationist. But whatever the apprehension and whatever the specific role assigned to an indigenous countervailing force to be developed, the economic weight of a united Western Europe has come to constitute the principal real pressure for Maghrebian unity. It has imposed on the anarchy of apparently universal freedom of political options the disciplining constraint of an economic necessity— to come to terms with the rising giant to the North, one way or another.

As a result, a question has been posed for Western Europe and for Western Europe and North Africa jointly. What kind of politics should govern the economics of the situation, or, more specifically, what more direct assistance toward unity might Western Europe adjoin to the indirect and unintended assistance emanating from the mere fact of her own economic integration? There seems to be a major choice open to the Western European powers in relation to North Africa. One major policy is to manipulate a competitive mobile equilibrium; another is to aim systematically at promoting an equilibrated unity. The first policy has an infinite number of variants on a single theme; the second encompasses three distinct approaches.

The policy of mobile equilibrium is apt to draw all major Western powers into North Africa and to make them act individually. Under such a more or less wittingly pursued policy, one or another North African state would be temporarily favored by one of the Western powers. The favorite would be expected to become a pilot country for the purposes of economic-development assistance and a conveyor belt for the popularity or political influence of the aiding power in parts of Africa less accessible to the donor. More or less deliberately, the North African states themselves would seek to play off the Western powers against each other, in an effort to get more advantage out of the protector of the moment or to exchange him for another, more profitable protector. As a result, Italy might come to specialize in Tunisia or Libya, as the most Mediterranean countries; West Germany might single out Algeria, as the economically most promising central country; and France would probably specialize in Morocco, as the most western and sentimentally congenial country, while trying to maintain a hold in Tunisia and Algeria. The United States would be drawn more deeply into North Africa; it would supplement Western European assistance or substitute for it during temporary crises, staking its hopes now on Tunisia, as the country best suited to become a model for development, now on Algeria, as the country most likely to be the political leader in North Africa and beyond, now on Morocco, as the country least likely to resort to radical socialist experiments for the time being.

Under the appearance of completing the political freedom of countries formerly tied to one power, the play-off policy is intrinsically colonialist. It would generalize the colonial policy of favoring apparently loyal or congenial groups against recalcitrant groups by extending it from groups to states and making it reciprocal. The policy pre-supposes that the North African system of states is and will remain an open one, unconfined in all directions, if only to facilitate the donor's political influence with the North African protégé being relayed to other African countries. The lack of confinement would probably inhibit the develop-ment of North African unity as a matter of uncoerced choice. While the policy could be pursued only as long as Algeria did not develop the capacity for regional hegemony, such hegemony might well be the unintended by-product of the policy. Algeria might be built up initially as a model coun-try or as core-power of a free and open North African as-sociation; but, once reinforced, she might actually choose to close the North African area to all Western influence, acting alone or in co-operation with a meanwhile economically strengthened Middle East Arab power or a Communist power.

By contrast, the second major policy would aim at co-ordinating the policies of the Western powers and anticipat-ing longer-term North African developments. Western Eu-ropean powers would have to share the economic and politi-cal advantages and liabilities of intimate links with the region, releasing American resources for employment else-where and enabling the North Africans to diversify their attachments within the Western European compass. Unless the Western European powers develop a united policy to-ward North Africa even before they are themselves fully united, they cannot promote North African unity to the point at which unity in the Maghreb might be safely per-fected in real or apparent temporary opposition to a united Europe (just as Europe's may have to be promoted in such an opposition to the United States).

The most delicate sharing is between France and West

Germany and Italy. France will be tempted again and again to cling to a bigamous relationship with Europe on one side and formerly French Africa on the other; but she will need just as repeatedly the assistance of her Western European partners in making her relations with her former dependencies mutually bearable. A special position for France in North Africa may help delay the maturing of some liabilities; these could, however, be more quickly disposed of by co-ordinated efforts. Increases in a joint aid for development and administrative purposes, for example, might be used for the compensation costs of converting colonial relationships into postcolonial ones. Such reconversion has so far mainly concerned agricultural colonization; but it might also involve the transfer of the French industrial presence from conspicuous sectors to less conspicuous and politically less sensitive postcolonial investments.

The initiatives that France or any other Western power can take are limited by at least two factors. The governments must enlist the co-operation of private economic interests; and a large degree of decolonization has already been achieved. But the prudent policy of the European Economic Community as an institution, to forego initiatives and to be merely receptive to bids for association by North Africans, can be usefully supplemented by a more active policy on the part of the member governments in favor of regional developments that would eventuate in some kind of connection between North Africa and Europe.

A formal association between North Africa and the European Economic Community is not for tomorrow; still less likely are joint defense arrangements. A considerable distance separates the Western Mediterranean defense schemes of the Gaillard and the de Gaulle governments; but it is probably less than the distance between the design and its realization. As the technological means of both destruction and dispersion develop, the military interest of Western Europe in association may decrease along with diminutions of the French military presence in the area. This might eventually improve the political climate for a new arrangement; but North Africa will first have to be decolonized materially and decolonize herself psychologically, learn to co-ordinate foreign and defense policies on a regional basis, and update her economic relationships with Western Europe. French cultural diplomacy in North Africa can meanwhile go on promoting the internalization of Western values without, hopefully, intensifying reactions to imperfect Western realities and without hoping that cultural links can substitute permanently for economic association in the middle run and politico-military association in the long run.

There are at least three ways of co-ordinating Western European policy toward North Africa in the future. All three are contrary to the play-off policy and involve a modification in current policy.

One approach is to employ assistance so as to promote regional co-operation directly. In such a case the Western powers would, among other things, adopt for the benefit of a North African politico-economic union the idea of industrial-mineral complexes at the Algero-Moroccan and Algero-Tunisian frontiers. The idea is not new. It was first envisaged in connection with a North African military-defense system to serve as a fall-back position for France and NATO; North African planners have subsequently embodied it in their functional design of a North African economic unity, developed in opposition to the European Common Market. An updated Western policy might sup-

port integration and specialization of productive functions
among the three countries while guaranteeing against abuses
of the special advantages that might accrue to a particular
country in a particular area of production. This might dis-
arm the issue of hegemony pending its sublimation in a
working association.

The second approach would aim at promoting regional
co-operation indirectly. Co-operation would grow as an incident to the bilateral relations of individual North African
countries with Western European countries or with the Common Market. The main requirement is to design the bilateral
relations so as to generate the kind of skills, resources, and
purchasing power that could be gradually brought into a
regional pool and stimulate expanding regional integration.
The third and last method would not promote a particular
design of economic unity. It would rather aim at creating
conditions under which unilateral political strategies of the
North Africans themselves might bring about unity. North
African countries would receive individualized assistance.
The assistance would not aim at developing complementary
specialized industries or at promoting the ramification of
lighter industries. It would, instead, aim at developing separate industrial and agricultural economies which would
heighten the economic viability of the individual countries
and which would be susceptible to precipitating merger as
an alternative to progressing competitiveness in a disintegrating regional political system.

The strategy-oriented policy would, in a way, have to
really make things worse before they could become really
better; it would differ from the policy of competitive play-
off by being co-ordinated among the Western powers and informed by a concept of the unification process, to be ad-

vanced by political and diplomatic means. The policy of creating conditions for indigenous strategy would express most accurately the limits of Western control over the utilization of Western assistance; like the policy of indirect support for regional unity, it would also express the current limits of the drive for unity in North Africa; and like the policy of direct support for such unity, it would reflect the limits of present readiness in North Africa for a formal association with Western Europe. The policy of merely promoting strategic possibilities for the future is political in the narrow or classic sense of politics as the imaginative manipulation of factors rather than organization; it demands, therefore, a particularly skillful approach to the political confinement of the unification universe as well as to the issues of equilibrium and hegemony among the countries to be united and authority within them.

The political confinement of the North African unification universe from the north and west is greater when the Western powers have a co-ordinated policy toward North Africa than if they do not. If the co-ordinated Western policy were to make assistance conditional on regional co-operation, moreover, the confinement would be greater than if the policy were merely conditioned by the sense of a unification strategy. In the latter case, confinement in other directions becomes crucial; too many escape possibilities from intra-regional competition or from a dynamic neighbor cannot but enfeeble reintegrative reactions to the threat of conflict and disintegration.

Perhaps fortunately for North Africa, confinement from east and south has been growing. The Sino-Soviet alternative is reduced whenever the Soviets are compelled to limit the resources expendable for a global policy and whenever the

Chinese live up to their campaign against aid to bourgeois regimes. The switch of the Algerians from Peking to Evian-les-Bains and from Havana to Washington soon after independence reflected rather accurately, moreover, the ambiguity in the attitude of the North African elites toward the Sino-Soviet option. They prefer most of the time that an Eastern flirtation soften up the West rather than harden into a break with the West. The behavior of FLN leaders could not but dampen the interest of China in Algeria, just as Moscow's concern for the feelings of Paris had before contained Russia's.

In the Middle East, the opening to Cairo is likely to be reduced, too. After a heady spell of messianic expansionism, Nasser has turned to socialism within and to more conventional and no more certainly successful power politics without. He may use kindred revolutionaries, or be used by them, in the name of unity, as he tries to push Egypt's influence along the Nile south of the Aswan dam into deeper Africa or as he follows the lure of oil-rich principalities and fertile crescents toward Asia. Both directions lead him away from the Maghreb, where unity can be sought in defense against Nasser or be justified as a preliminary to larger Arab unity, in a kind of dumbbell theory of all-Arab unification. Pan-Arabism as an effective force has appeared to be strongest in Algeria; it has been negated in Morocco by the link between Islamic traditionalism and territorially expansive Moroccan nationalism; and it has been virtually outlawed in Tunisia by its association with the underground opposition. It is unlikely that even Algeria would react to attempts to export Arab socialism westward any differently than Tunisia and Morocco reacted to Nasser's earlier attempts to transform Pan-Arabism from a weapon for independence into a handmaid of regional imperialism. The inclination of a socialist Algerian regime to establish an ideological alliance with Cairo would be unlikely to survive long the incompatibilities between western and eastern Arabs in general and between two potential core-powers of a larger association. Moreover, the Tunisians and the Moroccans would have once more a compelling reason to draw closer together in order to wean the Algerians lastingly away from Cairo back to the Maghreb.

In the South, finally, the latent incompatibility between so-called "negritude" and white Arabism, that has been coming into the open locally, may well transmute the honeymoon into a conflict between "new" Africa and the "greater" Arab Maghreb. The more reticent the Maghrebians are about conceding an effective part in the exploitation of the Sahara to the Black African littoral states, and the more grandiloquent they are regarding the economic possibilities of North Africa southward, the sharper will be the political reaction from the South. The so-called Casablanca Group might not be the only or the last casualty of basic differences in outlook and interests. All-African unity is a chimera, unless "unity" is read to mean no more than decolonization of an African system of states; or it is a slogan to cover up the hegemonic ambitions of particular leaders, perforce limited to less-than-continental proportions. A division of emancipated Africa along racial lines would, however, have none of the beneficial side effects of the continent's division into coherent regions or even of its fading division between militant neutralists looking eastward and non-aligned states leaning westward.

Unification in North Africa, while promoted by the narrowing of outlets southward, might well avert the consummation of a racial cleavage. It would open up new areas of effort within the Maghreb and keep open the more profitable avenues of trade and economic co-operation to the north, thus reducing incentives to economic penetration southward. Moreover, unity would reduce both incentive and opportunities for mixed Arab-Black African alignments over issues like Mauritania and the exploitation of the Sahara. Such alignments, while camouflaging the racial cleavage on the surface, would also exacerbate animosities in the longer run. A unified North Africa might, moreover, stimulate a broadly based process toward unity in Black Africa; this would complement the co-operative-competitive interactions between integrating units that already operate between Africa north of the Sahara and Europe north of the Mediterranean. Should the two major areas of Africa retain a comparable relationship to Western Europe, finally, the problem of intermediate countries like Mauritania and intermediate provinces like the Libyan Fezzan could not but be eased.

A radical solution to the problem of intermediate areas is territorial adjustment or, as it is put locally, *regroupement,* including partitions. In the past, partition schemes, leaving the so-called useful (i.e., economically endowed) parts of Algeria and Mauritania under French control were inspired by the interests of European colonizers and justified by the obligations of France to individual groups and her responsibilities for intercommunal equilibrium. The currently relevant equilibrium is a distribution of forces that would prevent one North African state from unifying the region coercively and that would instead promote regional unity through a measure of instability among freewheeling forces. The key local actors are Morocco and Algeria; Tunisia is a real if inferior weight and a potential intermediary, while Mauritania and Libya can alternately constitute weights for the Maghreb or buffers between the Maghreb and its African neighbors.

Mauritania and Libya are the countries best qualified to serve as connecting *traits d'union* between other countries, a role sought by virtually all others for themselves; but they are likewise countries most vulnerable to partitions. The forms and results of possible partitions and regroupings are unpredictable; and the trend might be hard to arrest before it affected Algeria and her neighbors. The wiser course is for Libya to keep out of the Maghreb association, at least provisionally, somewhat as Britain stayed out of the European one at a comparable stage. As long as the country keeps together, it can most usefully serve alternately as a desert path connecting the two main sections of the Arab caravan and as a sand curtain separating them when useful. As regards Mauritania, the preservation of the state need not, and probably should not, exclude concessions to the Moroccan viewpoint. Such concessions might have to comprise rectification of frontiers or extraterritorial arrangements at the expense of Algeria to give Morocco the presently lacking common boundary with Mauritania, facilitating political access. A composition of Moroccan claims would probably foster a balance of power in North Africa, more by releasing energies in the affected countries for constructive tasks than by enriching directly and immediately the Moroccan economy. The resources of the Moroccans might even be temporarily drained, if a species of personal union were supplemented or preceded by adjustments in the economic realm —for instance, by Morocco replacing France and the other Western powers as the main investor and aid distributor in the still less developed country.

Any such additional strain on the Moroccan economy would have to be eased from the outside. Total Western aid to North African countries should in any case be governed by concern for balance; an imbalance of local forces and external favors to them would tend to provoke drastic reactions on the part of the disfavored country. Whether the resources and the revenues originating in the Sahara can be distributed so as to help equilibrate the progress of the three countries toward greater economic strength depends on whether they will be distributed at all. The distribution may well turn out to be only an indirect one, if the Western powers and especially the Western European powers were to reduce assistance to Algeria in favor of the two wing countries as Algeria's revenues for development increase. Such an indirect distribution of Saharan revenues would serve the interest of fairness with regard to the past, since colonization curtailed territorially the two wing countries and Morocco in particular while enlarging Algeria; and it might serve the interest of equilibrium in the immediate future and of unity in the remoter one.

A shrinking of political options outside the region and controlled instability within it might well generate incidental gains in the realm of national authority. A reduction in the range of political distractions and an expansion of incentives to undertake constructive economic tasks might combine to reduce the practical significance of the differences in political style, leading personalities, and sources of authority that prevail in the countries of the Maghreb.

None of this could be injurious to the cause of independence in the Arab West and all of it might foster the cause of its unity. But little of this is likely to happen in time to avert deterioration, unless Western policy toward North Africa is co-ordinated. Otherwise, the East-West contest over North Africa might be followed or complicated by an intensified contest between the American and the European branches of the Atlantic alliance. A competitive involvement of the United States in North Africa is no more desirable than is such an involvement of Western European states in South America. It should not be impossible to obtain the co-operation of North Africans with a distribution of primary concerns among the Western powers; and it is mandatory to have them co-operate in keeping the Soviet Union out of North Africa at least until it admits Western Europe to a proportionate role in the Central-Eastern European portion of the larger Occident.

CHAPTER IV

A Renewed Europe in
Restored International Politics

The challenges with which North Africa confronts Western Europe are similar to the problems which the Western European countries face in all the less developed parts of the world as they are impelled to utilize and vindicate their growing economic strength. The relationships to be evolved between a uniting Western Europe and countries in Africa, Asia, and Latin America may be second in immediate importance to relationships with the United States and the Communist powers of Eurasia, but they are still important, if only because potentially distracting. On the one hand, the Western European powers will be tempted to pursue unilateral policies in the expectation that these will enhance their standing and supply them with new alternatives and leverages with which to increase their relative influence over the terms of European unity among other things. This tendency has been so far most striking in the case of France, as de Gaulle undertook once again to fuse in policy the several identities of France as a nation-state with a European vocation and as a universal idea imperfectly incarnate in world power. But the temptation is likely to spread as the Western Europeans respond in unanticipated ways to American pleas for a greater effort in the less developed countries. On the other hand, the dangers implicit in such a dispersion of effort, combined with the scale and the delicacy of the tasks, may on balance constitute a pressure in favor of co-ordinating both intra- and extra-regional policies. Only from a consolidated regional position can the Western European countries individually and as a group hope to nourish a world-wide *rayonnement* with the requisite blend of light and might in the long run.

If Western Europe is to resume definitively her place in the world, Europeans may now have to reverse priorities from intraregional to the external and global determinants of unity. This should not be impossible in a continent with a long tradition of primacy of foreign policy over internal politics. The reversal increases the interest of European unification for the student of world politics, just as it increases its hazards as well as its potentialities for the participants. The increases in hazards and in rightful expectations balance out when the undertaking conforms with the prevailing temper of international relations.

Half a century after the outbreak of World War I in Eastern Europe, the unification of Western Europe can be related to international relations in several ways. The unification process has absorbed some features of the approaches that were supposed to revolutionize international politics. The new regional unit is apt to benefit by the subtle changes that have actually occurred in international politics. And the comportment of a uniting Europe may reinforce traditional patterns of international politics.

Three Revolutions in International Politics

For some time now, legal-institutional, military, and economic factors have been successively cited in announcements of a new era of international politics. Only the economics of free trade in association with high finance was in a position to have a substantial although brief impact on international relations in the nineteenth century. Following World War I, the first revolution in international politics was proclaimed in the name of new law and institutions, and identified with the League of Nations. The succeeding revolutions fall into the period following World War II. They have been identified with nuclear-weapons technology and with the economics of functional integration and of phased development.

With each declared revolution an attempt has been made to impose concept on contingency, curb expediency with precept, and generally replace the unreliable rationality of political action in behalf of states with fundamentally novel strategies implementing normative or technical rationality. Normative rationality predominated in the strategy of collective security and peaceful settlement of disputes following World War I; technical emphasis came increasingly to the fore in strategies of thermonuclear deterrence and arms control, and in schemes for the deliberate creation of larger or new economic-political units, following World War II. These strategies were presumed to entail a division of labor between two kinds of powers: the principal producers of security, stability, and development and the principal consumers of such values. The division of labor was to take institutional form in permanent organizations which would supplement and gradually supersede the territorial state. To the extent possible, a rational administration and utilization of resources and a rational allocation of functions were to replace the dynamics of the territorial state system and a diplomacy responsive to circumstance and interest. In the guise of collective sanctions, all-out nuclear retaliation or economic assistance, more or less automatic responses to facts evaluated by objective criteria of misdemeanor or merit, were supposed to simplify international politics to the point of abolishing it altogether.

In reality, the working of an international system consisting of a number of competing power centers has warped the new strategies and designs. The grand new visions have had to be adjusted to the persistence of small-scale or devious coercion even more than to the threat of cataclysmic upheavals; in the process, they have assumed less radical proportions.

The proponents of an institutional revolution were the first to be disappointed, and on two occasions. The League of Nations, unable to supplant or to moderate traditional international politics, finally exacerbated it by acts of commission as well as omission. The later embodiment of a more cautious hope for the reordering of essential international relations toward greater simplicity and predictability of political behavior and its consequences has fared better only relative to the earlier failure. The reality was at first one of merely accidental collective action for security, transiently institutionalized; it has since become that of very elaborate, aptly improvised, but in no profound sense revolutionary, face-saving devices for disadvantaged contestants in inconclusive or marginal conflicts. Not unlike the League before, the United Nations has become less of an authoritative and more of a controversial and partisan organization with each of its metamorphoses, the brief spell of an apparently enhanced authority for the international executive notwithstanding.

The period following World War I witnessed abortive

attempts to restore classic economic and monetary international relationships under the safeguard of a novel politico-military order represented by the principles and the institutions of collective security. By contrast, the period surrounding the end of World War II witnessed a movement in favor of new techniques of regional economic reconstruction, integration, and development, only remotely related to the goal of a partial restoration of a liberalized global pattern, while traditional principles of an updated great-power concert were finding their way back into the half-heartedly restored military-political system of collective security. The flaw in the post-World War I order was the assumption that partial conflicts in a multipolar situation could be treated as if they were major hegemonial challenges polarizing the international system between assailants and defenders and suspending the play of particular political and economic interests for the duration of the threat. The comparable flaw in the post-World War II order was the attempt to stake the international security system ostensibly on the cohesion of a multipower directorate, while expecting to strengthen the long-term bases of peace and security by policies, such as those of economic promotion of secondary states, that are in practice the product of hegemonial great-power conflict and the contending parties' desire to gain and strengthen friends and allies.

The impetus of the Cold War made certain that functional economic co-operation would survive the end of interallied co-operation in World War II, even if in a different alignment. Such co-operation, along with economic-aid activities and the economic-growth race between the superpowers, has left a mark on contemporary international relations. But political considerations have tended to supplant the requirements of a new system of international relations that would implement the calculations of economic utility, whenever the new economics came into manifest conflict with old-style politics. This has been true in regard to initiation, phasing, and control of the integration of larger economic units as well as of the development of small, decolonized units of social and political organization. By and large, the economic factor has been overburdened by the militarily or politically stalemated powers, a situation which has invited abuse and tended to favor devious methods of reciprocal coercion rather than rationally co-ordinated joint efforts on the part of unequally developed states.

Breaches in the economizing approach have been especially painful in the most hopeful area for functional co-operation—that of the permanently organized peacetime coalition. Truly revolutionary potentialities inhere in the notion of a concerted division of defense functions and production tasks within integrated alliances of interdependent allies. These potentialities have, however, been sharply reduced by the reaffirmation of the political principle and the economic implications of independence, favoring parallel and no more than co-ordinated defense efforts. This development has been only one of several departures from the new international politics that was expected to result from the third and most spectacular revolution, the military-technological one.

The reappearance of war as an instrument of policy has upset the new politics' basic premise, the elimination of resort to force this side of Armageddon. The reintroduction of both conventional and highly unconventional, but non-nuclear, force on a limited scale was facilitated in practice by the manifest difference between nuclear and non-nuclear

weapons and the manifest reluctance of the nuclear powers
to engage in a direct and decisive contest. The restoration
of force to policy has been merely rationalized, for the purposes of the new science of international relations of thermonuclear deterrence, by *ex post facto* speculations about tacit
bargaining between adversaries in a test of strength (or,
by the notion's extension, in an arms race). The instances
of manifest self-limitation can, however, be adequately ex-
plained by nothing more novel or sophisticated than parallel
observance by the contestants in a local conflict of traditional legal and political inhibitions against overt intervention or flagrant provocation of already involved or still
uninvolved powers. The new rationality has been more original when linking again ultimate force and higher policy of
the major powers by way of particular nuclear strategies,
such as the deliberately controlled and selective counterforce strategy or even countercity strategy. The novelty in
procedure is apt to have a traditionalizing effect, however,
insofar as the strategy permits the political control and
exploitation of nuclear conflict.

   In a remote future the so far not so successful revolutions
may contribute to the making of fundamentally novel world
politics. Such a development would be, in part, a result of
the closing of unplanned time lags between normative ideas
and material conditions. Thus the legal-institutional revolution prepared normatively the ground both for the inhibitions
to war that have since ensued from the nuclear-weapons
revolution and for the material foundations of equality
among states that may yet evolve from the alleged capacity
of all states to develop in more or less predictable stages
and to aggregate into more or less expansive economies. The
politically motivated economic sanctions, promoted with in-

different results by proponents of the League of Nations, have since become relatively commonplace. They are being condemned as illicit strings by advocates of the more recently novel international politics of systematically promoted economic development. Increased vulnerability of the developing countries to economic sanctions may, however, eventually supplement other material conditions of an automatic system of general collective security, such as the diffusion of long-range nuclear weapons. Thus far, diffusion has been anathema to the proponents of the new international relations of thermonuclear stability, administered by the two superpowers.

For world politics to be truly transformed, political organization would first have to be consonant with the military means of destruction available to the most advanced states and with the economic means of construction available to the least developed portion of mankind as well as to the more advanced one. A new form of social and political order would consist of the division of the territorial nation-state into economically self-sufficient and militarily inefficient local units and the regrouping of these units in a preferably global organization. Nuclear technology would thus be mirrored in the social world. Elements of such a reorganization have been so far in evidence only in the ineffectual communalism of undeveloped countries and in the coercive communes of Communist China, on the local plane; and in the no more efficacious if less coercive organization of the United Nations, on the global plane. The regional unification of Western Europe may stimulate some moves toward local autonomy within the component countries by reducing the standing and the functions of the nation-state.

While not likely to be precursors of a type of organization

that would foster integrally new interunit politics, the Western European communities have embodied some features of the innovations that have thus far failed to revolutionize international politics. In the institutional and legal domains, the communities have imparted an effective role to judicial and international or even supranational decision-making institutions on a more than accidental and sporadic basis. In the economic domain, the functional integration of national economies in an enlarged market has been combined with some co-ordination of economic growth in unevenly developed areas and with liberalization of trade. And in the military domain, there has been a real prospect of exploiting the destructive potentialities of nuclear weapons for the establishment of political institutions susceptible of facilitating joint control over them. As European unification advances, however, these innovations are being transferred from the domain of international politics to the domain of intraregional and thus in a new sense internal politics.

Thermonuclear Stalemate and Dynamic Diplomacy

In the strictly international arena, a united Western Europe may benefit by some of the changes in international politics that have actually occurred, while helping to keep these changes limited. The principal changes that have occurred have arisen out of the existence of nuclear weapons, which has tended to intensify, formalize, and, if anything, expand the scope of diplomacy.

Diplomacy has been intensified, mainly in the relations between superpowers, as a result of an increased reluctance to resort to war. The traditional task of diplomacy is to find out whether it is possible or necessary to resort to war and to prepare the best possible conditions for waging war. Resort to the arbitrament of war or mere application of military pressures may suspend the workings of diplomacy or can actually supplement them, whenever parties to a conflict fail to agree on an estimate of yet unmobilized forces and already aroused interests of protagonists and possible allies. As overt force was reintroduced into the international politics of the Cold War, an apparently disarmed diplomacy has been sufficiently rearmed to assume most of its traditional tasks. These include prominently the manipulation of all available forms of military force. Given the nature of the new restraints in the invocation of ultimate force, stress has come to be placed upon the role of diplomacy in averting or terminating conflict. The task of preparing the best conditions for waging war in defense of vital interests has not been therefore abandoned; it merely has to be especially legitimized now by way of the real or pretended coincidence of measures of precaution against a still possible war with measures necessary for preventing an allegedly unthinkable war. No less than in the past, and possibly more so, diplomacy has had also to enact acute conflict and obtain limited political changes or (with greater efficacy) prevent undesirable major changes, by submitting the adversary to more or less authentic nuclear and non-nuclear military pressures.

One way of viewing the Cold War is to see it as a politico-military enactment of a World War III in thermonuclear conditions. It shares with the preceding two world wars the initially promising advance of the challenger, the checking of the advance in the central theater, an inconclusive diversion to non-European battlefields, and a reversion to the

European theater with meanwhile assembled material resources for the climacteric. The distinctive feature of the
latest global struggle has been the inability of any one party
to exact capitulation and impose terms. Diplomacy enters
warfare by way of military stalemate, however. Hence the
intermittent attempts to negotiate by word, symbolic deed,
or supporting pressure either suspensions of hostilities in
particular sectors of combat or separate peace settlements
with individual opponents. Such attempts are, in keeping
with the diplomacy of the earlier world wars of the eighteenth century among others, indistinguishable from attempts
to weaken the adversary alliance, to avoid the concessions
and compromises that make up a negotiated general peace
settlement, and to defer internal political disarmament that
might diminish the capacity for mounting or resisting a later
assault at the state system. Being indistinguishable from political war-making, the peace-making function of diplomacy
in wartime is fully compatible with the waging of pitched
battles by armed diplomacy, including nuclear diplomacy.
Pitched battles, such as those over Berlin and Cuba, take
place whenever the more aggressive side resorts to a surprise
move in an attempt to achieve a breakthrough in the military
or the political stalemate and has to be repulsed before militant peace-making can be resumed in a more muted key.

The wars of the mid-eighteenth century were waged on a
small scale, if only relative to some earlier and most later
wars. They may be compared, and must be contrasted, with
wars in the nineteenth and mid-twentieth century that have
been both small-scale and deliberately limited relative to
the resources available to the belligerents. The role of wartime diplomacy increases with desire or necessity to control
or limit the employed military force; diplomacy is galvanized

into still more intense activity when small-scale or large-scale, limited or unlimited, military forces are deadlocked. The contemporary equivalent of the typically stalemated wars of maneuver in the eighteenth century is, even more than a war like the Korean one, the politically controlled and motivated deployment of the likewise stalemated maximum weapons of our age, strategic nuclear weapons, in situations of crisis. Clausewitz's dictum about war being the *continuation* of political transactions with the admixture of other *means* has had to be rediscovered for a good reason. It was at variance with the doctrine of war stressing mass, mobility, and militarily decisive blows at the weak point of the enemy. The military strategy most congenial to a war conceived and conducted as an impetus behind political determinations is, by contrast, one of maneuver, elaborate in design but hampered in execution by socially or technologically induced restraints on impact or mobility that preclude an indisputable military decision. The ultimate identity of war and politics in general is one thing; the varied relationships of war and diplomacy are another. War that is, or can be, fought for military decision becomes properly a temporary *substitute* for particular political transactions, pending their being resumed with the admixture of intervening military *results*.

In both total and limited wars, including those of the twentieth century, fought with weapons and strategies that permit complete military victory of one side, limitation of political objectives has to be imposed by an act of enlightened political will. Even if the will is present, however, diplomacy will be inhibited as long as both sides anticipate favorable military developments. The scope of military activities and political objectives may be limited by the fear of expanding the conflict and involving popular emotions by way of mass mobilization, of diverting resources to what may be a subsidiary conflict, or of alienating needed diplomatic or military support. But the part of diplomacy directly related to the termination of a particular military conflict will be likewise limited by more or less long-lasting hopes for a favorable military outcome within the scope of the accepted military constraints. In conditions of stalemated military technologies and strategies, by contrast, diplomacy takes over as soon as the element of surprise in the initial moves has failed to overwhelm the principal opponent or disrupt the adversary coalition. Once only individual engagements can be won decisively but not the war itself, the adversary has to be isolated diplomatically rather than desolated militarily. The technologically imposed limitation on military goals that can be prudently envisaged dictates limitation of political goals that can be properly sought. These goals are unequivocally limited in regard to the main adversary; but they are in a sense unlimited in regard to the wartime diplomacy's primary target, the lesser allies of the principal adversary that are to be removed from the struggle or even induced to change sides. In this respect there is little fundamental difference between military confrontations of mercenaries with muskets and confrontations of technicians with missiles, between stalemates due to the inefficacy of weapons or strategies and those due to too efficacious weapons and too parlous and untested strategies, and between the related political strategies of dynasts, dictators, and strong democracies.

The diplomacy of the nuclear stalemate will only rarely raise overtly and explicitly the prospect of nuclear war. But it must always attempt to calculate the likely course and outcome of a hypothetical engagement and adjust both demands and pressures to the outcome of such calculations. The calculation may be unreliable, but it is intrinsically possible to the extent that it is based on the composition and deployment of available instruments of war at the critical moment. And the calculation is facilitated if the presumption against any one party securing a meaningful *military* victory is combined with the presumption against the momentarily favored contestant either exacting or claiming for himself a manifest *political* victory. More than ever, the crucial miscalculation concerns the kind and number of partial diplomatic and politico-military defeats a power can absorb before taking a final stand, rather than the military response of an adversary to major demands and provocations.

In these circumstances, Soviet Russia cannot rely on sheer military pressure to inhibit directly the process of political unification as long as the process is confined to Western Europe and, in fact, underwritten by the American nuclear guarantee; she depends on diplomatic means and inducements if she is to recover influence over developments in Western Europe. Conversely, and not least if it is eventually to extend to all of Europe, unification in Western Europe ought not to be pursued and implemented in ways that would preclude a symmetrical revision of the strategic military balance and prejudice the vital political interests of both the major power and the lesser states of Eastern Europe.

Once Western Europe is constituted as a unit, her standing as an actor in foreign politics is apt to be enhanced by a change that complements the intensification of diplomacy. This is the degree to which international politics has been formalized in the nuclear age. International politics is formalized to the extent that it is removed, without being separated, from the actual use of military or other material means of coercion. Diplomacy can be regarded as a formal activity interposed between foreign-policy objectives and the coercive, chiefly military, means available for attaining these objectives. The formalization of relations between two powers is increased when the willingness to resort to coercive means decreases on both sides and when the difficulties of communication between sides increase as a result of fundamental differences such as those of ideology. Formalization is not controverted by displays of calculated informality or even rudeness; formalism in international politics has become ever less a matter of the standard behavior of diplomats and ever more an impersonal aspect of crisis diplomacy as it approaches the danger zone of coercion. Nor is the new formalism limited to the greater rigor of hypothetical private calculations of the likely course of a military engagement as well as of a diplomatic crisis. Its main characteristics are, rather, refinement of styles and standardization of sequences in the interplay of demands and denials of demands between parties to succeeding crises.

Two developments have been associated with the formalization of diplomacy to the point of becoming an integral part of it. One has been the improvement in the modes of verbal and symbolic communication of interest, resolve, and moderation between the antagonists. Such communication is compounded of public statement, private communication, and meaningful act or reticence that both accompany and follow the truly serious confrontations between the nuclear superpowers. The other factor has been increased comprehension and at least tacit acceptance by the two superpowers of the broad outlines of their respective spheres of control or influence. The understanding and acceptance have, at least provisionally, extended to the limits of permissible rate of *asymmetrical* change in the configuration of these spheres by way of unsolicited intrusion into the sphere of the adversary. As a result fatal accidents and miscalculations have become less, not more, likely in the political domain at the present juncture, whatever may be true of the military-technological assurances against accidental war. The probability of the irreparable error is especially low, when partial failures in one geographic area can be offset by counteraction in another or be justified as means of demonstrating to the adversary the vulnerability of his control and to third parties the limits of aggressive nuclear diplomacy. The difference between the primitive and the evolved nuclear diplomacy is that between the activities attending and following the physical acts and ripostes of the first Berlin crisis and the Korean crisis on the one hand and, on the other hand, the verbal and symbolic communications that substituted for physical collisions in the second Berlin crisis and the Cuban crisis.

The situation is somewhat different in relations between major nuclear powers and minor nuclear or non-nuclear powers. In such relations, diplomacy as a formal activity interposed between the objectives of policy and the coercive means of policy is characterized less by a meticulous test of will than by calculated concessions of arrogated influence and importance to lesser states. The conceding powers are presumably superior enough to be able to make concessions, sufficiently inhibited from the employment of their power to be driven to making them, and sufficiently competitive to be attracted by the immediate advantages that favor of lesser states can bring. Among nuclear powers formalistic diplomacy has tended to be symbolic, expressing an under-lying capacity and the will to use the capacity in the last resort. In relations between major and minor powers, di-plomacy has tended to be fictional, in the sense of attributing function to lesser actors as if they possessed capacity. The function has been typically that of a mediator in great-power conflicts, if the minor power is non-nuclear as well as non-aligned; it becomes that of alternative party in great-power agreements or alignments if the lesser power is nuclear.

As she develops a nuclear capability of her own, Western Europe can expect to benefit from the formalization of rela-tions between unequal powers by enjoying an international role exceeding her material and, specifically, nuclear capa-bility. With the growth of this capability, Western Europe might contribute to the formalization of relations among roughly equal nuclear powers through the quality of her diplomatic action and as a result of the greater complexity and unpredictability introduced into international politics by the existence of more than two major nuclear powers. Most important, a unified Western Europe would not only further reduce the opportunities for unilateral gains presented by nuclear diplomacy, it would also promote the restora-tion of traditional forms of international politics.

Three Challenges in a Changing Balance of Power

By constituting a new superpower, a Western European regional union would contribute to the trend toward multi-polarity in the international system. A multipolar system has been in operation for some time with regard to actually usable power and effective influence, as distinct from continuing bipolarity with regard to large-scale, but severely inhibited, nuclear capabilities. The coexistence of rigid nuclear bipolarity and a relatively flexible system of multipolar politics has enhanced the role of instruments of conflict that can be regarded as functional substitutes for an unprofitable nuclear war, to the extent that they bring about transformations that would normally be sought by war. Here belong activities such as psychological propaganda warfare, foreign aid, United Nations diplomacy, economic-growth races, and outer-space explorations, some of which were originally regarded as basic features of radically novel international politics.

The rise of a strong Western European power would probably help to diversify and further expand such activities. And a strong Western Europe would contribute to placing such activities in a more realistic setting than has been the case so far. In relations between nuclear and non-nuclear powers, the capacity of a nuclear power to wage a general nuclear war and to win (in the sense of retaining an ability to act outside the national frontiers, while depriving the adversary of this ability) has not lost its importance. The capacity has actually been the precondition of the nuclear power being efficacious in a range of activities in the political, economic, and even cultural fields. But, on the part of the non-nuclear powers, the freedom to act, in the sense of exercising influence, has tended to take the place of a capacity to wield significant material resources as the criterion of international standing. As Western Europe develops limited but real capabilities, she is apt to close the political gap in regard to mobility and influence (to be distinguished from the gap in economic resources) that existed for some time between the new and weak states and the old and stronger states. Concurrently, she may help to redress the imbalance between the capacity to act forcefully and responsibly and the freedom to act independently at all. This imbalance has been the distorted reflection of nuclear stability and a potential factor of political instability in the world.

Progress toward redressing the imbalance would be speedier if the rise of Western Europe were to accentuate the shift toward a new dominant strategy of the contemporary conflict. The new strategy, of which there have been some inklings, is that of intensified diplomatic action among allies and between alliances, aiming at less rigid or exclusive configurations and alignments among relatively independent powers rather than at changes in the territorial status quo or in direct control over individual countries and governments. The shift would reduce to a largely instrumental and routinely performed role such hitherto dominant strategies of the Cold War as propagandistic conversion, sub-conventional subversion, and economic-aid warfare, all keyed to groups other than governments and to governments of states other than the well-established ones.

A change in the principal strategy might coincide with change in the identity of the most recent challengers of the established distribution of power and influence, including the measure of hegemony which the course and outcome of World War II conferred upon the United States. Soon there will have been three challenges to world political equilibrium since World War II. The first and continuing challenge has come from the U.S.S.R. The second was that of the underdeveloped countries in the mid-1950's. The third challenge is now arising from the renewed ancient states of Europe in the West and of Asia in the East.

As each successive power or grouping has advanced its policies and pretensions beyond its capabilities, it has been met by temporary and often tacit alignments between previous and later antagonists. The mechanism brought the Western powers, large parts of the underdeveloped world, and a small segment of the Communist world more closely together against the Soviet bloc. The same mechanism produced at least coincident patterns of resistance to the prominent role assumed by underdeveloped countries in world politics. While some in the West, notably the French and the British, opposed Afro-Asian domination of the UN, critics in the East, notably in China, resented the material and ideological costs of opportunistic Soviet activities in the Third World. In the immediate future, the mechanism may not only bring about an alignment of the superpowers with loyalists in the respective blocs against the insurgent elements within the disintegrating blocs; it may also produce a temporary rapprochement between the United States and the Soviet Union, brought closer together by parallel challenges to their view of regional order and provisional global stability following upon the failure of their successive efforts to ride the Afro-Asian wave toward a breakthrough into a congenial world order.

The equilibrium that has been in operation since World War II among the three main categories of states—the nuclear superpowers, the less developed new countries, and the renewed ancient powers—has had some features in common with the traditional balance of power. The party whose challenge has been partly or wholly repulsed has retreated into a role more proportionate to its capabilities. Even if this party retained its ambition to play a disproportionate role, it learned to moderate its methods in the direction of accepted conventions. Other aspects of postwar equilibrium have been contrary to balance-of-power politics. In the domain of international politics, the balance of power tended to polarize a multipolar system by way of a grand coalition against a major challenger. The contemporary equilibrium dynamic has tended instead to multilateralize the postwar bipolar system. This has happened as the successive bids for a disproportionate role produced mixed alliances and led to the build up of *ad hoc* allies on the one hand, and as the most forward powers separated themselves from their natural allies on the other.

In the domain of internal politics, moreover, bids for predominance in conditions of unlimited violence tended to promote trends toward authoritarian and even totalitarian systems. This was true under the traditional balance of power for the challenging countries, to some degree for Spain under Philip II, to a growing degree for France under Louis XIV and Napoleon, and on each of two occasions more fully for Imperial and Nazi Germany, as means were sought to harness all available resources for the effort that was as limited in available time as it was absolute in staked resources. By contrast, bids under conditions which permit no more than probing on a wide and shifting front have since seemed to promote moderation. Authoritarian or totalitarian states have sought to make the regime sufficiently attractive within and without to sustain a prolonged conflict. And representative regimes have not been propelled beyond an acceptable measure of strong authority toward a permanently mobilized and dictatorial garrison state.

Conclusions

A Diplomatic Pause and Long-Range Perspectives

The movement toward European unity has paused at the intersection between real or suspected hegemonial ambitions, unilateral exclusions, and bilateral connections. All of the principal parties to the unification process have joined the Soviet Union at one point or another as suspects of domineering ambition, resisted by potential partners unwilling to be the objects of such ambition. In an effort to avert Anglo-Saxon hegemony, France has been excluding Britain and, through her, the United States, while maintaining amiable bilateral relations with Britain, possibly as an alternative to the bilateral relationship with West Germany. Partly contrary to the French strategy, the United States has continued trying to keep the Soviet Union out of the unification process in Western Europe and the Atlantic area, while cultivating assiduous bilateral relations with the excluded power as an only half-consciously perceived potential check on unruly Western Europeans. The world of Afro-Asia, beset by very similar relationships in more than one of its regions, has moved to the sidelines, freed from European hegemony, unready to seriously contemplate imposing its own, and anxious to play the game of exclusions and shifting bilateral connections even without the sanction of an underlying constructive strategy.

163

The conspicuous pause in unification diplomacy has mirrored the still-concealed tension between the manifest nuclear-technological, and the latent geopolitical, determinants of basic policies and configurations. The requirements of the nuclear strategic balance have forced the United States and the Soviet Union together in mutual antagonism and common concern. The so-called negative community of interests between the two superpowers implies a countervailing alliance, however tacit and unholy, between impeded aspirants to nuclear status. France is closer in this respect to Communist China than she is to doubly allied West Germany, which, fearful of alienating one and provoking the other of the superpowers, has been hovering uncertainly between the respective risks and comforts of protected status and self-protection in regard to nuclear weaponry. But as policies designed to perpetuate an essentially bipolar nuclear-strategic pattern come seriously to inhibit third powers from converting their growing material assets into political dividends, the geopolitical determinant is likely to challenge ever more successfully the nuclear-military one. The shift between the two determinants will coincide with a crisis of widening options for some states and compulsions to avert undesired configurations for all states. The unfolding crisis is likely to shift Soviet attentions to the Western European grouping, as a means of averting a federative institutionalization of American presence in Western Europe and, worse still, the convergence of German and Chinese territorial aims and irredentist pressures on the Soviets' European and Asian domains.

As the structural preliminaries crystallize, conditions will ripen for adjustments in Central and Eastern Europe toward concurrent reunification of Germany and Europe as a whole in an initially only loose and precariously balanced system. Progress toward greater independence and unity in the region between Germany and Russia is indispensable for any working European system and concert; both autonomy and association may be facilitated by the conflict between the two major Communist powers and by the confinement of the area between Western Europe and the Soviet Union under circumstances that dampen the divisive force of traditional antagonisms. Calculated rigidity in tactics has a role to play in any sophisticated political strategy, however. A conspicuous increase in political or non-political contacts between West and East in Europe, especially if spearheaded by West Germany, would be worse than useless at this point; prematurely courting the few, the policy would but alienate the many.

The best way in which Western Europeans can work for a continental reconstruction is to move themselves toward unity along the lines of a regional, all-European, and global strategy. Such a strategy, we have noted, operates in the middle zone between completely free choice and outright coercion, as it seeks to compel a measure of unity by narrowing the range of available alternatives. Compulsion is least in evidence while political unity is being prepared, as it was in nineteenth-century Germany and has been in Western Europe, by functional co-operation which implements and promotes the convergence of concrete economic interests. When the unification process is to move into the political phase, the interests that must converge are those expressed in the fundamental foreign-policy options of the prospective members. A convergence of such options into an occasional association is always possible, and a particular set of conditions within and outside a region may make probable a more than tran-

sient coalescence; but purposeful strategy may be required
to relate conditions to designs and make some form of unity
appear necessary to governments naturally reluctant to sacri-
fice a range of options to a possibly irreversible commitment.

The success of a unification strategy that breaks up established patterns as a means of precipitating movement
toward new ones cannot but be problematic; so is the estimate
of the likely outcome. It is one thing to employ the strategy
to extend economic integration to a special sector, such as
the agricultural one, or to calculate the military forces and
political interests involved in an overt and brief struggle over
unity, such as the German one. It is quite another, more
difficult thing to precipitate even elementary political unity
with the aid of the wide range of structural and intangible
conditions of a global setting.

Despite stallings and setbacks, the strategy of unification,
as we have tried to explicate it, is not without supports and
prospects. Authorities in the prospective member-countries
are apparently consolidated and economic expansion on a
regional basis is likely to continue even if at a reduced rate;
the Common Market has contributed not only stimulating
incentives and confining bonds within the area of unification
but also a powerful leverage in relations with other powers.
The thermonuclear stalemate between the superpowers appears at once to require, and to create a sanctuary for developing, a separate European nuclear capability—a capability
that may be militarily useful even if it is not self-sufficient
and that may be necessary to spark the movement to political
unity even if it is developed concurrently with political advances at a later stage. The political domain proper displays
a not unfavorable combination of an elementary psychological and material equipoise among the Western European

countries, of disquieting Soviet-American contacts, of deepening Sino-Soviet cleavages, and, as regards the Afro-Asian countries, of pressures from disorderly ambitions and opportunities from rising economic needs and again declining political importance. All these developments ought to promote a progressive convergence of updated traditional foreign-policy options of prospective partners in Western European unity. And they ought to do so at a rate that will make the convergence coincide with and profit by the revival of classic diplomacy and the development of a new multipolar order in which the leading powers would work out the modalities of reciprocal access to areas adjoining the several heartlands.

An Exhortation from Exile

Unity in Western Europe, so far deputizing for all of Europe, has become a global event even before it has been consummated as a regional reality. The age-long interplay between Europe and the other parts of the world is entering upon a new phase. The interplay will take updated forms; but it will go on being marked by a mixture of imitation, antagonism, and reciprocal advantage.

The idea of supranational unity has been the latest in the stream of ideas which radiated from Europe abroad. The imitation has extended to the modes of implementing the idea, so far mainly by way of economic integration in common markets; and the familiar pattern of reception has been completed whenever the idea and the institution have been not only adopted as a model but also overstated even before the conditions of a beneficial realization were present. In the past, the adopted idea and partly deformed ideology have had a tendency to turn or be turned against their homeland. But, this time at least, the regeneration in Europe of the idea of unity has coincided with the return to Europe of another idea, that of independence. Transformed in the global crucible into that of decolonization, independence has largely liberated Western Europe from her colonial servitudes in the field of politics and economics and may be on the point of lifting her from a position of inferiority in the fields of defense and diplomacy. If it goes on materializing, the coincidence of unity and independence cannot but generate new power; and a new sense of power cannot but be reflected in a whole range of individual and collective achievements that thrive on the capacity of respected indigenous authority to value and to exploit such achievements.

The new power of Western Europe, like her unity, is perceived and even feared outside before it has been realized within, and before many Western Europeans have begun to sense it and even will it. The mixed feelings with which the stirrings of an independent Western European spirit have been greeted in the United States compare favorably with the animosity with which progress toward Western European unity and power has been received in large parts of the Communist world and the undeveloped world. The feelings are understandable and reach beyond apprehensions about markets and missiles. Just as the decline of Europe left a vacuum to be filled by others, so the rise of Western Europe inevitably marks positions to be surrendered again. The surrender will not be least painful when it bears on the intangibles of prestige, influence, and leadership in implementing the idea of supranational unity in such a way as to conserve and restore what is worth conserving and restoring.

The dualism of European politics, expressed in the tension between the national and the supranational principles, can also be stated as that of power and norm. The present danger for European unity is that West Europeans will fail to relate norm to power, design to strategy, as long as they regard Western Europe from within, as a marketplace for economic and political transactions, and not also from without, as a military and diplomatic base for wider reconstruction. A utopian stress on design thrives best in the atmosphere of impotence. This fact explains the emphasis on design in the first postwar phase of European unification, when Western Europe as a whole was weak. And the fact accounts for some of the more recent behavior of minority parties and factions, faced with governments pre-empting the feasible and attractive political ideas, and the behavior of ruling statesmen in the lesser states, faced with the strategy-minded leader of a greater power.

It may have been possible at some time to make a new Europe by novel means and for such a Europe to inspire the world with the example of a new international or supranational politics. But the possibility has waned for the time being with the gradual subsidence of the international system into traditional patterns of political action. In the not so new world that is re-emerging from the liquidation of two world wars and several global empires, Western Europe now faces the more pressing task of acting as a unity toward the outside, even before she constitutes an integrated unity within, and of acting externally as a power even while she is only being consolidated as an institution and an idea. The internal political and economic costs of the strategic phase of European unification are not negligible; neither are the foreign-policy risks. They are acceptable only insofar as the historically tested underlying principles are sound and the particular facts of international politics conform to the supporting general view of the contemporary international system. What is acceptable in the truly great and inescapable challenges to statecraft, however, has a way of being at once necessary and worthy of undertaking.

The options at fateful turning points are few and the failure to embrace any of them fully carries the worst penalty. More forcefully than anyone else before or after, a patriot dwelt upon this cardinal rule of statecraft as he ransacked the past in order to help restore the future of Italy, another embattled fragment of the state system in need of unity, in the days following the disappearance of the "gleam of hope . . . that an individual might have been appointed by God for her redemption. . . ." The melancholy phrase, from the last chapter of *The Prince,* continues: ". . . yet at the summit of his career he was cast aside by fortune, so that now, almost lifeless, she awaits someone to heal her wounds. . . ." Italy had to wait the better part of four centuries for another Machiavellian, Cavour, to be another age's more successful Cesare Borgia. Some Europeans may prefer not to owe great historic transformations to individuals inclined to either fashion events like Caesars, however liberally, or allow nothing else to be, however diplomatically. But, still without a proven substitute for the consummating deed, they may usefully go on pondering the intimation in Machiavelli's final exhortation from virtual exile—that opportunities, if they are passed up, tend to pass away; and that smiling fortune, if ignored, spurns in return.

Selected Bibliography

Chapter I. The World after a Half-Century

BINKLEY, ROBERT C. *Realism and Nationalism, 1852–1871.* New York, 1935.

COURT, W. H. B. *A Concise Economic History of Britian: From 1750 to Recent Times.* Cambridge (England), 1954.

DEHIO, LUDWIG. *Germany and World Politics in the Twentieth Century.* New York, 1960.

DORN, WALTER R. *Competition for Empire, 1740–1763.* New York, 1940.

HENDERSON, W. O. *The Industrial Revolution on the Continent: Germany, France, Russia, 1800–1914.* London, 1961.

LANGER, WILLIAM L. *European Alliances and Alignments, 1871–1890.* New York, 1950.

———. *The Diplomacy of Imperialism, 1890–1902.* New York, 1951.

MARDER, A. J. *From the Dreadnought to Scapa Flow,* Vol. I. *The Road to War 1904–1914.* London, 1961.

MARTIN, LAURENCE W. (ed.). *Neutralism and Nonalignment. The New States in World Affairs.* New York, 1962.

TAYLOR, A. J. P. *The Struggle for Mastery in Europe, 1848–1918.* Oxford, 1954.

TEMPERLEY, HAROLD. *The Victorian Age in Politics, War, and Diplomacy.* Cambridge (England), 1928.

Chapter II. The Conditions of European Unity

ATIYA, AZIZ S. *Crusade, Commerce and Culture.* Bloomington, 1962.

BARK, WILLIAM CARROLL. *Origins of the Medieval World.* Stanford, 1958.

COULBORN, RUSHTON. (ed.). *Feudalism in History.* Princeton, 1956.

DARMSTAEDTER, F. *Bismarck and the Creation of the Second Reich.* London, 1948.

DAWSON, CHRISTOPHER. *The Making of Europe: An Introduction to the History of European Unity.* London, 1932.

DENIAU, JEAN FRANÇOIS. *The Common Market.* New York, 1960.

DEUTSCH KARL W., *et al. Political Community and the North Atlantic Area: International Organization in the Light of Historical Experience.* Princeton, 1957.

ERDMANN, CARL. *Die Entstehung des Kreuzzugsgedanken.* Stuttgart, 1935.

EYCK, ERICH. *Bismarck and the German Empire.* London, 1950.

FERRERO, GUGLIELMO. *The Reconstruction of Europe: Talleyrand and the Congress of Vienna, 1814–1815.* New York, 1941.

HAAS, ERNST B. "International Integration: The European and the Universal Process," *International Organization,* Summer, 1961.

KISSINGER, HENRY A. *A World Restored: Metternich, Castlereagh and the Problem of Peace, 1812–1822.* Boston, 1957.

KITZINGER, U. W. *The Challenge of the Common Market.* Oxford, 1962.

KOHN, HANS, (ed.). *German History: Some New German Views.* London, 1954.

LISKA, GEORGE. *International Equilibrium* (Chapter 6. "The Pattern of Integration."). Cambridge, Mass., 1957.

MAYNE, RICHARD. *The Community of Europe.* London, 1962.

MORGENTHAU, HANS J. and HUTTON, GRAHAM. "The Crisis in the Western Alliance: Two Views," *Commentary,* March, 1963.

MOSSE, W. E. *The European Powers and the German Question, 1848–1871.* Cambridge (England), 1958.

PHILLIPS, W. A. *The Confederation of Europe: A Study of the European Alliance, 1813–1823.* London, 1920.

STRAYER, JOSEPH R. *Western Europe in the Middle Ages: A Short History.* New York, 1955.

WEBSTER, SIR CHARLES. "The Council of Europe in the Nineteenth Century," *The Art and Practice of Diplomacy.* New York, 1962.

Chapter III. A United Europe in a Divided World

ALLEN, H. C. *The Anglo-American Predicament: The British Commonwealth, the United States and European Unity.* New York, 1960.

BARBOUR, NEVILL. *A Survey of North West Africa.* London, 1959.

BERQUE, JACQUES. *Le Maghreb entre deux guerres.* Paris, 1962.

BRUNSCHWIG, HENRI. *Mythes et réalités de l'impérialisme colonial français, 1871–1914.* Paris, 1960.
EHRHARD, JEAN. *Le destin du colonialisme.* 3rd ed. Paris, 1958.
FANON, FRANTZ. *Les damnés de la terre.* Paris, 1961.
DE GAULLE, CHARLES. *War Memoirs.* 5 vols. New York, 1955–60.
HOAG, MALCOLM W. "Nuclear Policy and French Intransigence," *Foreign Affairs,* January, 1963.
JULIEN, CHARLES-ANDRÉ. *Histoire de l'Afrique du Nord: Tunisie, Algérie, Maroc.* 2nd ed., 2 vols. Paris, 1951–52.
KISSINGER, HENRY A. "NATO'S Nuclear Dilemma," *The Reporter,* March 28, 1963.
LE TOURNEAU, ROGER. *Evolution politique de l'Afrique du Nord musulmane, 1920–1961.* Paris, 1962.
LISKA, GEORGE. *Nations in Alliance: The Limits of Interdependence.* Baltimore, 1962.
DE ROSE, FRANÇOIS. "Atlantic Relationships and Nuclear Problems," *Foreign Affairs,* April, 1963.
SPINELLI, ALTIERO. "Atlantic Pact or European Unity," *Foreign Affairs,* July, 1962.
ZAGORIA, DONALD S. *The Sino-Soviet Conflict, 1956–1961.* Princeton, 1962.
ZARTMAN, I. WILLIAM. "The Sahara—Bridge or Barrier?," *International Conciliation,* January, 1963.

Chapter IV. A Renewed Europe in Restored International Politics

CLAUDE, INIS L., JR. *Power and International Relations.* New York, 1962.
HERZ, JOHN H. *International Politics in the Atomic Age.* New York, 1959.
LISKA, GEORGE. *International Equilibrium: A Theoretical Essay on the Politics and Organization of Security.* Cambridge, Mass., 1957.
———. *The New Statecraft: Foreign Aid in American Foreign Policy.* Chicago, 1960.
MILLIKAN, MAX F. and BLACKMER, DONALD L. B. (eds.). *The Emerging Nations: Their Growth and United States Policy.* Boston, 1961.
MORGENTHAU, HANS J. *Scientific Man vs. Power Politics.* Chicago, 1946.
OSGOOD, ROBERT E. *Limited War: The Challenge to American Strategy.* Chicago, 1957.

POLANYI, KARL. *The Great Transformation.* New York, 1944.
SCHELLING, THOMAS C. and HALPERIN, MORTON H. *Strategy and Arms Control.* New York, 1961.
TUCKER, ROBERT W. *The Just War: A Study in Contemporary American Doctrine.* Baltimore, 1960.

INDEX

Absorption, in internal affairs: as condition of concert, 40–41, 43; contrasted with economic expansion, 46

Adenauer, Konrad: successors to, 100

Africa: and Western Europe, 7, 118; and the balance of power, 107; relations between North and South, 123, 126, 137–38; unity schemes in, 127, 137; racial problem in, 137–38. *See also* Afro-Asia; North Africa

Afro-Asia: relation to Europe, 13–14, 20, 117, 118, 168; international role of, 13–16, 18–20, 159–60, 161, 163; development of, 16–17, 20; regional unification in, 18, 20; relation to Western Europe, 142, 167; communalism in, 149

Algeria: relation to France, 119, 124; and regional unity, 121–22, 126, 127, 133; and intraregional conflicts, 124; authority in, 125; and regional equilibrium, 125–26, 131, 138–40; and extraregional powers, 126, 130, 131, 136–37. *See also* Sahara

Alignments: adaptations of, 114–16; as stake of Cold-War strategy, 160; determinants of, 164. *See also* Foreign policy

Anglo-Saxon powers: and French foreign-policy options, 68-69; and West Germany, 69, 81. *See also* Great Britain; United States

Arms races: characteristics of, 11–12; control of, 112, 113; and tacit bargaining, 148

Atlantic Community: evolutionary possibilities of, 102–3; anticipation of, 105. *See also* North Atlantic Treaty Organization

Austria, Imperial: internal development of, 16; and France, 19, 68; and German unification, 50, 52, 57, 63, 78, 97; foreign-policy experiences of, 81. *See also* Austria-Hungary

Austria-Hungary: and political concert, 40; and Triple Alliance, 79; and Dual Alliance, 114, 119. *See also* Austria, Imperial

Authority: divisions in, 22–23, 31; as condition of unification, 29–30, 31–32, 46–49, 124–25, 140, 166; transfer of, 30; in contemporary societies, 67, 162

Balance of power: mutations in, 8–9, 20, 103–4, 106–7, 160–62; and political organization, 23, 34, 35, 146; and internal politics, 67, 162; British role in, 69, 72, 107; American concern over, 84. *See also* Bipolarity; Equilibrium

Bavaria: and German unification, 53, 97

Berlin crises: general implications of, 152, 157

Bipolarity: loosening of, 103–4, 115, 117, 160; consequences of retightening of, 117–18; in nuclear weapons, 159

Bismarck, Prince Otto von: parliamentary struggles of, 48; unification strategy of, 52–53, 55, 62–63; compared with de Gaulle, 65–66, 76, 111, 119; evaluation of, 65–66, 76–77, 78; attitude to federal institutions, 76; international statecraft of, 110–11

Borgia, Cesare: and Italian unity, 170

Briand, Aristide: and plan for United States of Europe, 48, 58

Byzantine empire: and the Christian West, 24, 28, 32. *See also* Church, Greek Orthodox

Carolingian empire: and Papacy, 24, 25; and Islam, 44

Index